# Recipe remix

**Woman's Day**

# Recipe remix

## Start with 1 basic recipe, get 4 delicious dishes

by Kate Merker and the editors of *Woman's Day*

HEARST BOOKS

New York

# Foreword

 In the 21 years I've been cooking for my family, a lot has changed. Gone are the no-kid days when dinner was a multicourse ritual; also behind me are the baby and toddler years, where mac 'n' cheese and chicken nuggets were the meal of choice. Now we're in the insanely-crazy-busy years, when the four of us eating together is a minor miracle, and meals have to be quick and easy. And not involve chicken nuggets.

So I appreciate a good shortcut, one that will get our food to the table with a minimum of fuss. Consider *Recipe Remix* an important tool in your arsenal. The premise is simple: You start with one basic recipe, which can then become many others. So the chicken breasts you buy in bulk (for a whole lot less) can be marinated with orange and rosemary, or rubbed with spices, or glazed with honey and soy sauce, before being grilled. Or master an easy recipe for pancakes, then try four variations, both savory and sweet (mmm!, apple pie pancakes with maple walnuts!).

These easy little shortcuts add up to a lot of time saved in the kitchen, so you can focus less on cooking and more on what's really important: being together. Enjoy!

*Susan*

Susan Spencer
EDITOR-IN-CHIEF, *WOMAN'S DAY*

# Introduction

We've all been there at some point. You get home at 6:30 P.M. and have to pull dinner together with the contents of the fridge. There's food in there, but you just can't see how any of those ingredients (half a bunch of spinach, chicken breast, the dregs of various condiment jars, leftover rice and a couple of wilting scallions) can come together to create a meal that your family will love. It's taken me a lot of time, practice and experimentation to get here, but now I can whip up mustard chicken with spinach rice that's been flavored with sautéed onions and scallions while making it look effortless.

Early on in my culinary education, I discovered that repetition made the difference. I would work on the same skill or technique or dish over and over again until it became second nature to me. I started with simple proteins. Once I mastered seared chicken breast, then I would try grilling it, followed by roasting and so on. Then I would change the cut and do the same thing all over again. After that I worked on developing the taste. I played with herbs, spices and other various flavors and combinations until it was a hit. And then I would move on to the rest of the meal, figuring out what I could add to make it a delicious and satisfying dinner.

In developing the concept of *Recipe Remix* for the magazine and subsequently curating its articles for this book, you'll see that my culinary adventures have continued, but they now take place in many different kitchens, not just my own. I have a terrific team of people who join me in creating, tasting and tweaking recipes in the *Woman's Day* test kitchen. Together our goal is not only to provide you with many new recipes, but also to help you feel more comfortable with the idea of just whipping something up. Master one recipe, then mix it up on your own. Drop one ingredient here, add another that you have on hand, and a whole new recipe is born.

I hope that the recipes on the following pages will not only help you in those moments when you're caught staring into the fridge, but will also inspire you to switch things up every once in a while. Great cooking comes from lots of practice, and having a few remixes up your sleeve.

Happy cooking,

*Kate*

Kate Merker
FOOD & NUTRITION DIRECTOR, *WOMAN'S DAY*

p14

p17

p28

p27

p20

p19

p31

p12

p24

# Breakfasts, Brunches & Lunches

# Scramble it up

It's easy to get a meal on the table if you crack a few eggs! Hearty breakfasts or quick dinners are only 20 minutes away.

**START HERE**

## BASIC SCRAMBLED EGGS

**ACTIVE** 10 MIN • **TOTAL** 10 MIN • **SERVES** 4 • COST PER SERVING 34¢

8    large eggs
     Kosher salt and
     pepper
1    Tbsp olive oil or
     unsalted butter

1 In a large bowl, whisk together the eggs, 1 Tbsp water and ½ tsp each salt and pepper.
2 Heat the oil or melt the butter in a 10-in. nonstick skillet over medium heat. Add the eggs and cook, stirring every few seconds with a rubber spatula, to desired doneness, 2 to 3 minutes for medium-soft eggs.

PER SERVING 174 CAL, 13 G FAT (3.5 G SAT FAT), 372 MG CHOL, 382 MG SOD, 13 G PRO, 1 G CAR, 0 G FIBER

### 1 *Pimiento cheese & ham scramble*

**ACTIVE** 15 MIN • **TOTAL** 15 MIN
**SERVES** 4
COST PER SERVING $1.11

Whisk together the egg mixture as directed, adding 1 to 2 tsp **hot sauce**. Heat 1 Tbsp **olive oil** in a large nonstick skillet over medium heat. Add 3 oz thinly sliced **deli ham** (torn into small pieces) and cook, tossing occasionally, until beginning to brown around the edges, 2 to 3 minutes. Add 1 medium **roasted red pepper** (cut into ¼-in. pieces) and cook, tossing, for 1 minute; transfer to a plate. Add the egg mixture to the skillet and cook as directed. Fold in the ham and pepper, 2 **scallions** (thinly sliced), ½ cup coarsely grated **extra-sharp Cheddar** and 2 Tbsp **cream cheese** (cut into small pieces).

PER SERVING 292 CAL, 21 G FAT (8 G SAT FAT), 407 MG CHOL, 819 MG SOD, 20 G PRO, 4 G CAR, 1 G FIBER

## 2 *Kielbasa, potato & onion scramble*

**ACTIVE** 25 MIN • **TOTAL** 25 MIN • **SERVES** 4 • COST PER SERVING $1.28

Whisk together the egg mixture as directed. Heat 2 Tbsp **olive oil** in a 10-in. nonstick skillet over medium heat. Add 8 oz **Yukon Gold potatoes** (cut into ½-in. pieces) and cook, covered, stirring occasionally, for 8 minutes. Add 1 small **onion** (chopped) and cook, covered, until the potatoes are golden brown and tender, 4 to 5 minutes more. Add 6 oz **kielbasa** (thinly sliced on a diagonal) and cook, uncovered, tossing occasionally, until golden brown, about 5 minutes; transfer the potato mixture to a plate. Add the egg mixture to the skillet and cook as directed. Fold in the potato mixture, ½ cup coarsely grated **Pepper Jack cheese** and ½ cup **fresh flat-leaf parsley** (chopped).

PER SERVING 412 CAL, 28 G FAT (9 G SAT FAT), 417 MG CHOL, 987 MG SOD, 23 G PRO, 15 G CAR, 1 G FIBER

### 3 Mushroom, spinach & Gruyère scramble

**ACTIVE** 20 MIN • **TOTAL** 20 MIN • **SERVES** 4
COST PER SERVING $2.28

Whisk together the egg mixture as directed. Heat 1 Tbsp **olive oil** in a large skillet over medium heat. Add 1 medium **onion** (chopped) and ¼ tsp each **salt** and **pepper** and cook, covered, stirring occasionally, until very tender, about 8 minutes. Increase the heat to medium-high, add 8 oz small **cremini or white mushrooms** (quartered) and cook, tossing occasionally, until golden brown and tender, 4 to 5 minutes. Meanwhile, cook the egg mixture in a 10-in. nonstick skillet as directed. Add 4 cups **spinach** (roughly chopped) to the eggs and cook, folding, until beginning to wilt. Fold in the mushroom mixture and 4 oz **Gruyère cheese** (coarsely grated; about 1 cup).

PER SERVING 351 CAL, 26 G FAT (9 G SAT FAT), 403 MG CHOL, 626 MG SOD, 24 G PRO, 7 G CAR, 2 G FIBER

### 4 Asparagus, mint & Parmesan scramble

**ACTIVE** 15 MIN • **TOTAL** 15 MIN • **SERVES** 4
COST PER SERVING $1.23

Whisk together the egg mixture as directed. Heat the oil or melt the butter in a 10-in. nonstick skillet over medium heat. Add ½ lb **asparagus** (sliced into ½-in.- thick pieces) and cook, stirring occasionally, until beginning to soften, 3 to 4 minutes. Add the egg mixture and cook as directed. Remove from the heat and fold in ½ cup finely grated **Parmesan** and ¼ cup fresh **mint** (chopped).

PER SERVING 231 CAL, 16 G FAT (5 G SAT FAT), 381 MG CHOL, 544 MG SOD, 18 G PRO, 4 G CAR, 2 G FIBER

# Plenty of pancakes!

These creative mix-ins and toppings are so yummy you'll never settle for just syrup again.

**START HERE**

## BASIC BUTTERMILK PANCAKES

**ACTIVE** 15 MIN • **TOTAL** 15 MIN • **SERVES** 4 (MAKES 12 4-IN. PANCAKES) • COST PER SERVING 33¢

| | |
|---|---|
| 1½ | cups all-purpose flour |
| 2 | Tbsp granulated sugar |
| 1 | tsp baking powder |
| ½ | tsp baking soda |
| ½ | tsp kosher salt |
| 2 | large eggs |
| 1½ | cups buttermilk |

**1** In a large bowl, whisk together the flour, sugar, baking powder, baking soda and salt. In a separate bowl, whisk together the eggs and buttermilk. Add the buttermilk mixture to the flour mixture, whisking to combine (a few small lumps are fine).

**2** Heat a large nonstick skillet over medium-low heat. Check the heat by sprinkling it with water—when the water evaporates immediately, pour 3 scant ¼ cups of batter into the skillet.

**3** Cook the pancakes until bubbles begin to appear at the edges and in the center, 1 to 2 minutes. Using a spatula, peek under the pancakes. When they are golden brown, carefully flip them.

**4** Cook the pancakes 1 minute more. Peek to make sure the underside is golden brown, transfer them to a baking sheet and cover loosely with foil to keep warm. Repeat with remaining batter to make 12 pancakes (if your pancakes stick, wipe the skillet with 1 tsp canola oil before cooking the next batch).

PER SERVING 270 CAL, 4 G FAT (1 G SAT FAT), 97 MG CHOL, 669 MG SOD, 11 G PRO, 47 G CAR, 1 G FIBER

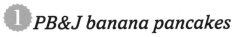

# 1. PB&J banana pancakes

**ACTIVE** 20 MIN • **TOTAL** 20 MIN • **SERVES** 4 • COST PER SERVING 58¢

Prepare the basic buttermilk pancakes with the following changes: Increase the **sugar** to ¼ cup. Omit the buttermilk. Whisk ½ cup **creamy peanut butter** into the **eggs** with 1 cup **whole milk**. Stir 1 **banana** (sliced) into the batter before cooking; cook as directed. In a small skillet, whisk together ½ cup **strawberry jam** and 2 Tbsp **water**. Warm over medium heat (adding an extra tsp water if the jam is too thick). Serve with the pancakes along with extra sliced bananas, if desired.

PER SERVING 609 CAL, 21 G FAT (5 G SAT FAT), 99 MG CHOL, 746 MG SOD, 18 G PRO, 91 G CAR, 4 G FIBER

## ② Ham & pea pancakes with chive butter

**ACTIVE** 25 MIN • **TOTAL** 25 MIN
**SERVES** 4 • COST PER SERVING $1.19

Prepare the basic buttermilk pancakes with the following changes: Stir 8 oz **ham** (diced) and 1 cup **frozen peas** (thawed) into the batter. Cook as directed. Serve with chive butter: Combine 4 Tbsp **unsalted butter** (at room temperature) with 1 to 2 Tbsp chopped **fresh chives**.

PER SERVING 459 CAL, 17 G FAT (9 G SAT FAT), 153 MG CHOL, 1,278 MG SOD, 23 G PRO, 54 G CAR, 3 G FIBER

## ③ Apple pie pancakes with maple walnuts

**ACTIVE** 20 MIN • **TOTAL** 20 MIN
**SERVES** 4 • COST PER SERVING $1.37

Prepare the basic buttermilk pancakes with the following changes: Increase the **sugar** to ¼ cup and add 1 tsp **apple pie spice** to the flour mixture. Stir 1 **apple** (peeled and diced) into the batter before cooking. Cook as directed (using 2 Tbsp batter each for silver dollar pancakes). Serve with maple walnuts: Simmer ½ cup **maple syrup** and ⅛ tsp **salt** in a small saucepan over medium heat until slightly thickened, about 5 minutes. Mix in ½ cup **heavy cream** until fully incorporated, then simmer for 1 minute. Stir in ½ cup toasted **walnuts** (roughly chopped).

PER SERVING 605 CAL, 23 G FAT (9 G SAT FAT), 138 MG CHOL, 746 MG SOD, 14 G PRO, 88 G CAR, 3 G FIBER

## ④ Orange cornmeal pancakes with honey, oranges & almonds

**ACTIVE** 20 MIN • **TOTAL** 20 MIN
**SERVES** 4 • COST PER SERVING 50¢

Prepare the basic buttermilk pancakes with the following changes: Increase the **sugar** to ¼ cup, add ¾ cup **yellow cornmeal** to the flour mixture, and add 1 Tbsp grated **orange zest** to the eggs and buttermilk. Cook as directed. Serve with sliced **oranges**, **honey** and toasted sliced **almonds**.

PER SERVING 405 CAL, 4 G FAT (1 G SAT FAT), 97 MG CHOL, 671 MG SOD, 13 G PRO, 77 G CAR, 3 G FIBER

# A slice above

Any one of these takes on quiche will
fit the bill for breakfast, lunch or dinner.

START
HERE

## BASIC HERB QUICHE

**ACTIVE** 15 MIN • **TOTAL** 1 HR • **SERVES** 8 • COST PER SERVING 72¢

| | |
|---|---|
| 1 | refrigerated rolled pie crust |
| 2 | tsp olive oil |
| 1 | large onion, finely chopped |
| | Kosher salt and pepper |
| ¾ | cup fresh flat-leaf parsley, chopped |
| 4 | large eggs |
| ¾ | cup sour cream |
| ½ | cup whole milk |
| ¼ | tsp freshly grated nutmeg (optional) |
| 4 | oz Gruyère or Swiss cheese, grated (1 cup) |

❶ Heat oven to 425°F. Fit the pie crust into and up the sides of a pie plate; fold the edge of dough underneath itself to create a thicker ½-in. border that rests on the lip of the plate and crimp as desired. Place on a rimmed baking sheet and bake until lightly golden, 12 to 15 minutes. Remove and reduce oven heat to 375°F.

❷ Meanwhile, heat the oil in a large skillet over medium heat. Add the onion and ¼ tsp each salt and pepper and cook, stirring occasionally, until soft, 5 to 7 minutes. Stir in the parsley and remove from heat.

❸ In a large bowl, whisk together the eggs, sour cream, milk, ¼ tsp each salt and pepper, and nutmeg, if using. Gently stir in the onion mixture and Gruyère.

❹ Pour the egg mixture into the crust. Bake until just set and a knife inserted in the center comes out clean, 35 to 40 minutes. Let rest for 5 minutes before serving.

PER SERVING 268 CAL, 19 G FAT (9 G SAT FAT), 122 MG CHOL, 369 MG SOD, 10 G PRO, 16 G CAR, 1 G FIBER

## ①Smoked ham, leek & Gruyère quiche

**ACTIVE** 15 MIN • **TOTAL** 1 HR • **SERVES** 8
COST PER SERVING $1.00

Follow the basic herb quiche instructions, substituting 2 medium **leeks** (white and light green parts only; chopped) for the onion and 2 tsp **fresh thyme** for the parsley. With the sour cream and milk, whisk in 1 Tbsp **Dijon mustard**. Lay 4 oz thinly sliced **deli ham** in the bottom and up the sides of the baked quiche shell, pour in the egg mixture and bake as directed.

PER SERVING 297 CAL, 21 G FAT (9 G SAT FAT), 130 MG CHOL, 610 MG SOD, 12 G PRO, 17 G CAR, 0 G FIBER

## ②Roasted asparagus & goat cheese quiche

**ACTIVE** 15 MIN • **TOTAL** 1 HR • **SERVES** 8
COST PER SERVING $1.36

Follow the basic herb quiche instructions, omitting the onion and parsley. On a rimmed baking sheet, toss ½ lb **asparagus** (trimmed and cut into 1-in. pieces), 1 Tbsp **olive oil** and ¼ tsp each **salt** and **pepper**. Roast on the oven rack underneath the quiche shell until just tender, 6 to 8 minutes. Add the asparagus to the egg mixture along with 4 sliced **scallions** and 2 Tbsp chopped **mint leaves**. Substitute 4 oz crumbled fresh **goat cheese** for the Gruyère and bake as directed.

PER SERVING 250 CAL, 18 G FAT (8 G SAT FAT), 113 MG CHOL, 373 MG SOD, 8 G PRO, 15 G CAR, 1 G FIBER

## ③ *Onion, pepper & feta quiche*

**ACTIVE** 15 MIN • **TOTAL** 1 HR • **SERVES** 8
COST PER SERVING 95¢

Follow the basic herb quiche instructions, adding
1 medium thinly sliced **bell pepper** along with
the onions. Sauté, stirring occasionally, until the
vegetables are tender, 6 to 8 minutes; stir in the
parsley. Substitute 4 oz crumbled **feta** for the Gruyère
and bake as directed.

PER SERVING 252 CAL, 18 G FAT (8 G SAT FAT), 120 MG CHOL, 480 MG SOD,
8 G PRO, 17 G CAR, 1 G FIBER

## ④ *Italian sausage, tomato & Cheddar quiche*

**ACTIVE** 20 MIN • **TOTAL** 1 HR 5 MIN • **SERVES** 8
COST PER SERVING 96¢

Follow the basic herb quiche instructions, adding 6
oz **Italian sausage** (casings removed) to the sautéed
onions, and cook, breaking it up with a spoon, until no
longer pink, 4 to 5 minutes. With the parsley, stir in 1
cup **grape tomatoes** (halved). Substitute 4 oz  **extra-
sharp Cheddar** for the Gruyère and bake as directed.

PER SERVING 347 CAL, 26 G FAT (12 G SAT FAT), 138 MG CHOL, 568 MG SOD,
12 G PRO, 16 G CAR, 1 G FIBER

# Make it melted

Behold, the five greatest grilled cheese sandwiches you've ever tasted.

**START HERE**

## BASIC GRILLED CHEESE

**ACTIVE** 10 MIN • **TOTAL** 15 MIN • **MAKES** 2 • COST PER SERVING $1.21

- 4    thick slices country or Pullman bread
- 1    Tbsp unsalted butter, melted, or olive oil
- 4    oz Cheddar, coarsely grated

**1** Brush one side of each slice of bread with butter or oil. Form sandwiches (buttered-side out) with the cheese.

**2** Heat a large nonstick skillet over low heat. Cook the sandwiches, covered, until the bread is golden brown and crisp and the cheese has melted, 4 to 5 minutes per side.

**PER SERVING** 511 CAL, 28 G FAT (15.5 G SAT FAT), 75 MG CHOL, 858 MG SOD, 20 G PRO, 43 G CAR, 2 G FIBER

## 1 *Ham & pimiento grilled cheese*

**ACTIVE** 10 MIN • **TOTAL** 15 MIN
**MAKES** 2 • COST PER SERVING $1.79

Butter or oil the bread as directed. Form sandwiches with the **Cheddar**, 2 Tbsp **lowfat cream cheese**, ½ tsp **hot sauce** (optional), 2 thin slices **deli ham**, 2 Tbsp **jarred sliced pimientos** (drained) and 1 **scallion** (thinly sliced). Cook as directed.

**PER SERVING** 579 CAL, 32 G FAT (17.5 G SAT FAT), 90 MG CHOL, 1,064 MG SOD, 22 G PRO, 45 G CAR, 3 G FIBER

### 2 Roast beef & French onion grilled cheese

**ACTIVE** 10 MIN • **TOTAL** 45 MIN • **MAKES** 2 • COST PER SERVING $1.87

Heat 1 Tbsp **olive oil** in a medium skillet over medium heat. Add 1 small **onion** (sliced), season with ¼ tsp each **salt** and **pepper** and cook, covered, stirring occasionally, for 12 minutes. Reduce the heat to medium-low, stir in 1 tsp **fresh thyme leaves** and cook, uncovered, stirring occasionally, until the onions are golden brown, 15 to 20 minutes more (add 1 Tbsp water to the skillet if the onions start sticking). Butter or oil 4 slices **rye bread** as directed. Form sandwiches with the bread, 1 Tbsp **whole-grain mustard**, 2 oz **Gruyère** (coarsely grated) and 2 slices thinly sliced **roast beef**. Cook as directed.

PER SERVING 430 CAL, 25 G FAT (11 G SAT FAT), 64 MG CHOL, 840 MG SOD, 21 G PRO, 31 G CAR, 4 G FIBER

### ❸ Pear & Gouda grilled cheese

**ACTIVE** 10 MIN • **TOTAL** 15 MIN • **MAKES** 2
COST PER SERVING $2.10

Butter or oil the bread as directed.
Form sandwiches with the bread,
1 Tbsp **Dijon mustard**, 4 oz **Gouda**
(coarsely grated), 1 **pear** (thinly
sliced) and 1 cup **arugula**. Cook
as directed.

PER SERVING 460 CAL, 23 G FAT
(14 G SAT FAT), 80 MG CHOL, 991 MG SOD,
20 G PRO, 44 G CAR, 6 G FIBER

### ❹ Pepperoni, spinach & mozzarella grilled cheese

**ACTIVE** 10 MIN • **TOTAL** 15 MIN • **MAKES** 2
COST PER SERVING $1.29

Split 2 **ciabatta rolls** in half and
brush the outsides with melted
butter or oil. Form sandwiches with
the rolls (buttered-sides out), 2 Tbsp
**marinara sauce**, 4 oz **mozzarella**
(coarsely grated), 1 oz thinly
sliced **pepperoni** and 1 cup **baby
spinach**. Cook as directed.

PER SERVING 544 CAL, 27 G FAT (13 G SAT FAT),
75 MG CHOL, 1,214 MG SOD, 28 G PRO, 50 G CAR,
3 G FIBER

# Picnic perfect

These combos are simple to pull together as a lunch or make-ahead dinner. Try them piled high on bread or paired with a green salad.

**START HERE**

## BASIC CHICKEN SALAD

**ACTIVE** 5 MIN • **TOTAL** 35 MIN • **SERVES** 4 • COST PER SERVING $1.03

Kosher salt and pepper

1½ lb boneless, skinless chicken breasts

¼ cup lowfat sour cream

2 Tbsp mayonnaise

2 scallions, thinly sliced

½ cup fresh flat-leaf parsley, chopped

❶ Fill a medium saucepan halfway with water; bring to a boil and add 1 tsp salt. Add the chicken, reduce heat and gently simmer until cooked through, 10 to 12 minutes. Transfer the chicken to a plate. When cool enough to handle, shred or cut into pieces.

❷ In a large bowl, whisk together the sour cream, mayonnaise and ½ tsp each salt and pepper. Add the chicken and toss to coat. Fold in the scallions and parsley.

PER SERVING 253 CAL, 9 G FAT (2 G SAT FAT), 103 MG CHOL, 474 MG SOD, 40 G, PRO, 3 G CAR, 1 G FIBER

**❶ *Southwestern chicken salad***

**ACTIVE** 10 MIN • **TOTAL** 40 MIN
**SERVES** 4
COST PER SERVING $1.44

Prepare the chicken. Prepare the dressing, adding 3 Tbsp **fresh lime juice** and 2 tsp **chili powder**; toss with the chicken. Add a 15-oz can **black beans** (rinsed) and 1 cup **corn kernels** (fresh or frozen and thawed) and mix to combine. Fold in the scallions, and substitute **cilantro** for the parsley.

PER SERVING 385 CAL, 10 G FAT (2 G SAT FAT), 103 MG CHOL, 740 MG SOD, 47 G PRO, 29 G CAR, 9 G FIBER

## 2 Chicken salad with apples & radishes

**ACTIVE** 10 MIN • **TOTAL** 40 MIN • **SERVES** 4
COST PER SERVING $1.49

Prepare the basic chicken salad, omitting the parsley. Add 4 **radishes** (cut into thin half-moons), 2 stalks **celery** (thinly sliced) and 1 small **green apple** (quartered and thinly sliced) and mix to combine. Fold in 1 cup **watercress** or **baby arugula**.

PER SERVING 275 CAL, 9 G FAT (2 G SAT FAT), 103 MG CHOL, 504 MG SOD, 40 G PRO, 9 G CAR, 2 G FIBER

## 3 Chicken salad with carrots, mustard & tarragon

**ACTIVE** 10 MIN • **TOTAL** 40 MIN • **SERVES** 4
COST PER SERVING $1.26

Prepare the basic chicken salad, omitting the parsley. Prepare the dressing, adding 1 Tbsp **Dijon mustard** and 1 Tbsp **whole-grain mustard**; toss with the chicken. Fold in the scallions, 2 medium **carrots** (coarsely grated) and 1 Tbsp **fresh tarragon** (chopped).

PER SERVING 276 CAL, 9 G FAT (2 G SAT FAT), 103 MG CHOL, 748 MG SOD, 40 G PRO, 7 G CAR, 1 G FIBER

## 4 Curried chicken salad

**ACTIVE** 10 MIN • **TOTAL** 40 MIN • **SERVES** 4
COST PER SERVING $1.17

Prepare the basic chicken salad. Prepare the dressing, adding 2 Tbsp **fresh lemon juice** and 1 Tbsp **curry powder**; toss with the chicken. Fold in the scallions and ½ cup **raisins**; omit the parsley.

PER SERVING 319 CAL, 9 G FAT (2 G SAT FAT), 103 MG CHOL, 473 MG SOD, 41 G PRO, 20 G CAR, 2 G FIBER

p68

p72

p82

p59

p34

p60

p67

p46

p41

# Dinners

# Fire it up!

Simple chicken breasts turn into something special with a little added flavor and flame.

START HERE

## BASIC GRILLED CHICKEN

**ACTIVE** 15 MIN • **TOTAL** 15 MIN • **SERVES** 4 • COST PER SERVING 99¢

**4  6-oz boneless, skinless chicken breasts**

**Kosher salt and pepper**

**Olive oil, as needed**

**1** Heat grill to medium-high. Clean the grill and lightly oil.

**2** For marinated chicken, season with ½ tsp salt and ¼ tsp pepper before grilling. For chicken that is glazed or topped with a sauce or relish, rub with 2 tsp oil before seasoning with salt and pepper.

**3** Grill all the chicken until cooked through or an instant-read thermometer inserted into the thickest part of the breast registers 165°F, 4 to 6 minutes per side.

### **1** *Grilled chicken with nectarine, red onion & basil relish*

**ACTIVE** 15 MIN • **TOTAL** 20 MIN
**SERVES** 4
COST PER SERVING $1.52

In a medium bowl, whisk together ¼ cup **olive oil**, 2 Tbsp **white wine vinegar** and ¼ tsp each **salt** and **pepper**. Add 2 ripe **nectarines** or **peaches** (thinly sliced) and ½ small **red onion** (thinly sliced) and toss to combine. Oil, season and grill the **chicken** as directed. Fold ½ cup **fresh basil** (chopped) into the nectarine mixture and spoon over the chicken.

PER SERVING 361 CAL, 20 G FAT (3 G SAT FAT), 94 MG CHOL, 445 MG SOD, 35 G PRO, 9 G CAR, 2 G FIBER

## 2 *Sweet apple & mustard marinated grilled chicken*

**ACTIVE** 15 MIN • **TOTAL** 35 MIN • **SERVES** 4
COST PER SERVING $1.39

In a large bowl or resealable plastic bag, combine ¼ cup each **whole-grain mustard** and **apple juice**, 2 Tbsp **cider vinegar** and ½ cup fresh **flat-leaf parsley** (chopped). Add the **chicken** and marinate for 20 minutes. Remove the chicken from the marinade (discard the marinade). Season and grill the chicken as directed.

**PER SERVING** 191 CAL, 4 G FAT (1 G SAT FAT), 94 MG CHOL, 401 MG SOD, 35 G PRO, 1 G CAR, 0 G FIBER

## 3 *Spice-rubbed grilled chicken*

**ACTIVE** 15 MIN • **TOTAL** 15 MIN • **SERVES** 4
COST PER SERVING $1.25

In a small bowl, combine 1 Tbsp **ground cumin**, 1 tsp **curry powder**, ½ tsp **ground ginger**, ½ tsp **salt** and ⅛ tsp **cayenne pepper**; stir in 1 Tbsp **olive oil**. Rub the spice mixture on the **chicken** and grill as directed (omit the salt and pepper).

**PER SERVING** 222 CAL, 8 G FAT (2 G SAT FAT), 94 MG CHOL, 326 MG SOD, 35 G PRO, 1 G CAR, 1 G FIBER

## ④ *Orange & rosemary grilled chicken*

**ACTIVE** 15 MIN • **TOTAL** 35 MIN • **SERVES** 4
COST PER SERVING $1.43

In a large bowl or resealable plastic bag, combine 2 tsp **orange zest**, ¼ cup **fresh orange juice**, 2 Tbsp **fresh lime juice**, 2 cloves **garlic** (thinly sliced) and 1 Tbsp **fresh rosemary** (chopped). Add the **chicken** and marinate for 20 minutes. Remove the chicken from the marinade (discard the marinade). Season and grill the chicken as directed.

**PER SERVING** 187 CAL, 4 G FAT (1 G SAT FAT), 94 MG CHOL, 323 MG SOD, 34 G PRO, 1 G CAR, 0 G FIBER

## ⑤ *Sticky Asian-glazed grilled chicken*

**ACTIVE** 15 MIN • **TOTAL** 15 MIN • **SERVES** 4
COST PER SERVING $1.39

In a small bowl, combine ½ cup **ketchup**, 2 Tbsp each **honey** and **low-sodium soy sauce**, and 1 Tbsp each **chili powder** and grated **fresh ginger**. Oil, season and grill the **chicken** as directed, basting with the sauce during the last 3 minutes of cooking.

**PER SERVING** 276 CAL, 7 G FAT (1 G SAT FAT), 94 MG CHOL, 958 MG SOD, 36 G PRO, 18 G CAR, 1 G FIBER

# Beyond basic mac 'n' cheese

You never knew this comforting classic could taste even better.

**START HERE**

## BASIC MACARONI & CHEESE

**ACTIVE** 30 MIN • **TOTAL** 40 MIN • **SERVES** 6 • COST PER SERVING $1.69

| | |
|---|---|
| 1 | lb elbow macaroni |
| 1 | Tbsp olive oil, plus more for the baking dish |
| 1 | medium onion, finely chopped |
| | Kosher salt and pepper |
| 1 | clove garlic, finely chopped |
| 1 | Tbsp all-purpose flour |
| 1½ | cups whole milk |
| 4 | oz lowfat cream cheese |
| ¼ | tsp freshly grated or ground nutmeg |
| ⅛ | tsp cayenne pepper |
| 8 | oz extra-sharp Cheddar, shredded (2 cups) |
| 8 | oz Gruyère, shredded (about 2 cups) |

❶ Heat oven to 425°F. Oil a shallow 3-qt baking dish or six 2-cup ramekins. Cook the pasta according to package directions.

❷ Meanwhile, heat 1 Tbsp oil in a large skillet over medium-low heat. Add the onion, ¾ tsp salt and ¼ tsp pepper and cook, covered, stirring occasionally, until very tender, 8 to 10 minutes. Stir in the garlic and cook for 1 minute. Sprinkle the flour over the onion mixture and cook, stirring, for 1 minute.

❸ Whisk in the milk and bring to a simmer. Whisk in the cream cheese, nutmeg and cayenne until blended. Stir in the Cheddar and Gruyère and simmer, stirring occasionally, until the cheese is melted and the mixture is slightly thickened, 1 to 2 minutes.

❹ Toss the pasta with the cheese sauce and transfer to the prepared baking dish. Bake until golden brown, 10 to 12 minutes.

**PER SERVING** 531 CAL, 26 G FAT (14 G SAT FAT), 74 MG CHOL, 548 MG SOD, 25 G PRO, 48 G CAR, 2 G FIBER

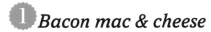 **1** *Bacon mac & cheese*

**ACTIVE** 45 MIN • **TOTAL** 55 MIN • **SERVES** 6 • COST PER SERVING $1.97

Prepare the basic macaroni and cheese recipe, substituting 2 **leeks** (cut into ½-in.-thick half-moons) for the onion. In a small bowl, toss the 6 slices **bacon** (cooked, cooled and broken into small pieces) with 1 cup **fresh bread crumbs**, ½ cup **fresh flat-leaf parsley** (chopped), 1 Tbsp **olive oil** and ¼ tsp each **salt** and **pepper**. Sprinkle over the macaroni and cheese and bake as directed.

**PER SERVING** 603 CAL, 31 G FAT (15 G SAT FAT), 80 MG CHOL, 782 MG SOD, 28 G PRO, 53 G CAR, 3 G FIBER

## ② *Cajun mac & cheese*

**ACTIVE** 45 MIN • **TOTAL** 50 MIN • **SERVES** 6
COST PER SERVING $2.32

Prepare the basic macaroni and cheese recipe, cooking 1 **green bell pepper** (sliced) along with the onion. Omit the nutmeg and cayenne and stir in 2 tsp **Cajun seasoning** (no salt added). Thinly slice a 13-oz package of **kielbasa**. Heat 1 Tbsp **olive oil** in a large skillet over medium-high heat. Brown the kielbasa, about 1 minute per side. Fold into the pasta mixture and bake as directed.

**PER SERVING** 655 CAL, 36 G FAT (17 G SAT FAT), 106 MG CHOL, 1,236 MG SOD, 31 G PRO, 51 G CAR, 2 G FIBER

## ③ *Tex-Mex mac & cheese*

**ACTIVE** 40 MIN • **TOTAL** 50 MIN • **SERVES** 6
COST PER SERVING $2.21

Prepare the basic macaroni and cheese recipe, substituting 8 oz **Pepper Jack cheese** for the Gruyère. Whisk in ¾ cup **salsa verde** (green salsa) along with the cream cheese. Before transferring to the baking dish, fold in 2 cups shredded **rotisserie chicken**, 1 cup **fresh corn kernels**, 2 **plum tomatoes** (roughly chopped) and 1 cup **fresh cilantro leaves**. Bake as directed.

**PER SERVING** 622 CAL, 29 G FAT (15 G SAT FAT), 104 MG CHOL, 924 MG SOD, 34 G PRO, 54 G CAR, 3 G FIBER

## ④ *Reuben mac & cheese*

**ACTIVE** 40 MIN • **TOTAL** 50 MIN • **SERVES** 6
COST PER SERVING $2.51

Prepare the basic macaroni and cheese recipe, whisking in 3 Tbsp **Dijon mustard** along with the cream cheese. Before transferring to the baking dish, fold in 8 oz **sauerkraut** (drained and squeezed of excess moisture) and 8 oz sliced **deli corned beef** (thinly sliced). Tear 4 slices **rye bread** (crusts removed) into ½-in. pieces. Toss with 1 Tbsp **olive oil** and ¼ tsp each **salt** and **pepper**. Sprinkle over the pasta mixture and bake as directed.

**PER SERVING** 628 CAL, 29 G FAT (15 G SAT FAT), 89 MG CHOL, 1,213 MG SOD, 32 G PRO, 58 G CAR, 4 G FIBER

# Super soup

With these four chicken cure-alls,
there's year-round comfort in a bowl.

START HERE

## BASIC CHICKEN SOUP

**ACTIVE** 15 MIN • **TOTAL** 1 HR • **SERVES** 6 • COST PER SERVING $2.13

2   bone-in chicken
    breast halves
    (about 2 lb total)

3   medium carrots,
    sliced ¼ in. thick

2   stalks celery, sliced
    ¼ in. thick

1   medium onion,
    quartered and
    sliced crosswise

2   32-oz containers
    (8 cups total) low-
    sodium chicken
    broth

    Kosher salt and
    pepper

**1** Place the chicken, carrots, celery and onion in a large pot. Add the broth, cover and bring to a boil.

**2** Reduce heat, add ¾ tsp salt and ½ tsp pepper and simmer, covered, until the chicken is cooked through and the vegetables are tender, 15 to 20 minutes (skim and discard any foam that rises to the top).

**3** Transfer the chicken to a bowl. When cool enough to handle, shred the meat, discarding the skin and bones. Stir the chicken back into the soup and cook until heated through, about 3 minutes.

♥ **PER SERVING** 215 CAL, 7 G FAT (3 G SAT FAT), 73 MG CHOL, 520 MG SOD, 29 G PRO, 7 G CAR, 2 G FIBER

## ❶ *Chicken soup with smoked sausage, white beans & greens*

**ACTIVE** 25 MIN • **TOTAL** 1 HR 10 MIN
**SERVES** 6 • COST PER SERVING $2.89

Make the classic chicken soup. Meanwhile, cut 6 oz **fully cooked Italian chicken sausage** links into ¼-in.-thick slices. Heat 1 Tbsp **olive oil** in a large skillet over medium-high heat and brown the sausage, 1 to 2 minutes per side. Add the sausage to the soup along with 1 small head **escarole** (torn into 2-in. pieces, about 6 cups) and a 15-oz can **white beans** (rinsed). Simmer until the escarole is tender, 4 to 5 minutes.

**PER SERVING** 358 CAL, 11 G FAT (3 G SAT FAT), 95 MG CHOL, 1,139 MG SOD, 40 G PRO, 24 G CAR, 7 G FIBER

### ③ *Asian chicken noodle soup*

**ACTIVE** 25 MIN • **TOTAL** 1 HR 10 MIN
**SERVES** 6 • COST PER SERVING $2.83

Prepare the classic chicken soup, adding a 2-in. piece **fresh ginger** (sliced ½ in. thick) to the pot along with the chicken, vegetables and broth. Cook as directed; remove and discard the ginger. Meanwhile, cook 6 oz **rice noodles** according to package directions, then stir them into the soup. Serve with 2 cups **bean sprouts**, 1 **jalapeño** (thinly sliced), 1 cup **fresh cilantro**, **lime wedges** and Asian or other **hot sauce**.

♥ **PER SERVING** 333 CAL, 7 G FAT (3 G SAT FAT), 73 MG CHOL, 526 MG SOD, 31 G PRO, 36 G CAR, 3 G FIBER

### ② *Sweet potato & couscous chicken soup*

**ACTIVE** 20 MIN • **TOTAL** 1 HR 5 MIN • **SERVES** 6
COST PER SERVING $2.49

Prepare the classic chicken soup, omitting the carrots and replacing them with 1 lb **sweet potatoes** (peeled and cut into ½-in. pieces). Add ¼ cup **tomato paste** and ½ tsp each **ground cumin** and **smoked paprika** to the pot along with the chicken, vegetables, and broth; cook as directed. When adding the shredded chicken to the pot, also stir in a 15-oz can **chickpeas** (rinsed) and ¼ cup **couscous**. Simmer for 3 minutes.

**PER SERVING** 338 CAL, 8 G FAT (3 G SAT FAT), 73 MG CHOL, 643 MG SOD, 34 G PRO, 30 G CAR, 5 G FIBER

### ④ *Lemon chicken & rice soup*

**ACTIVE** 25 MIN • **TOTAL** 1 HR 10 MIN • **SERVES** 6
COST PER SERVING $2.31

Make the classic chicken soup. Meanwhile, cook ½ cup **long-grain white rice** according to package directions. In a medium bowl, whisk 3 large **eggs** and ¼ tsp **salt** until frothy. Whisk in ¼ cup fresh **lemon juice**. Whisking constantly, gradually add 1 cup of the hot chicken soup (liquid only) to the egg mixture. Gradually whisk in an additional cup of soup. Stir in ¼ cup chopped **fresh flat-leaf parsley**. Stir the egg-soup mixture and rice into the soup in the pot; warm for 2 minutes (do not let it simmer or boil).

**PER SERVING** 315 CAL, 10 G FAT (3 G SAT FAT), 166 MG CHOL, 639 MG SOD, 34 G PRO, 21 G CAR, 2 G FIBER

# Master marinara

Modify this simple red sauce to fit
your family's tastes with delicious mix-ins,
from sausage to shrimp.

## BASIC MARINARA

**ACTIVE** 25 MIN • **TOTAL** 1 HR 30 MIN • **MAKES** 12 CUPS • COST PER SERVING $1.15

¼  cup olive oil

2  large onions, finely
chopped

2  medium carrots,
grated

Kosher salt and
pepper

8  cloves garlic, finely
chopped

¼  cup fresh oregano,
chopped

4  28-oz cans whole
plum tomatoes

❶ Heat the oil in a large pot over medium heat.
Add the onions, carrots, 1 tsp salt and ½ tsp
pepper and cook, stirring occasionally, until very
tender and beginning to brown, 15 to 20 minutes.

❷ Add the garlic and oregano and cook, stirring,
for 2 minutes (do not let it brown).

❸ Add the tomatoes and their juices, squashing
the tomatoes with your hands as you add them
to the pot; bring to a boil. Reduce heat and
simmer, stirring occasionally, until thickened,
45 to 55 minutes.

**PER ½ CUP SERVING** 154 CAL, 2 G FAT (0 G SAT FAT), 0 MG CHOL,
371 MG SOD, 1 G PRO, 8 G CAR, 1 G FIBER

##  Shrimp puttanesca fettuccine

**ACTIVE** 25 MIN • **TOTAL** 25 MIN • **SERVES** 4
COST PER SERVING $3.60

Using a vegetable peeler, remove 4 strips of **zest** from a **lemon**; thinly slice the zest. Heat 2 Tbsp **olive oil** in a large skillet over medium-high heat. Season 1 lb **large peeled and deveined shrimp** with ¼ tsp **salt** and cook, tossing occasionally, for 3 minutes. Add ½ cup **Kalamata olives** (halved), 1 Tbsp **capers** and the lemon zest and toss to combine. Add 2 cups **marinara** and simmer until the sauce is heated through and the shrimp are opaque throughout, about 4 minutes. Toss with 12 oz cooked **fettuccine** or other long pasta.

**PER SERVING (WITH PASTA)** 550 CAL, 15 G FAT (2 G SAT FAT), 143 MG CHOL, 1,446 MG SOD, 29 G PRO, 74 G CAR, 5 G FIBER

## ② Eggplant, basil & fresh mozzarella penne

**ACTIVE** 30 MIN • **TOTAL** 30 MIN • **SERVES** 4
COST PER SERVING $2.13

Heat 3 Tbsp **olive oil** in a large nonstick skillet over medium heat. Add 1 medium **eggplant** (cut into ½-in. pieces), season with ¼ tsp each **salt** and **pepper**, and cook, stirring occasionally, until golden brown and tender, 12 to 15 minutes. Add 2 cups **marinara** and simmer until heated through, about 3 minutes. Remove from heat and stir in ½ cup **fresh basil** (torn) and 4 oz **bocconcini** (small balls fresh mozzarella; halved). Toss with 12 oz cooked **penne** or other short pasta.

♥ **PER SERVING (WITH PASTA)** 560 CAL, 19 G FAT (5 G SAT FAT), 20 MG CHOL, 516 MG SOD, 19 G PRO, 79 G CAR, 9 G FIBER

### ③ *Spicy mushroom & parsley linguine*

**ACTIVE** 30 MIN • **TOTAL** 30 MIN • **SERVES** 4
COST PER SERVING $2.33

Heat 3 Tbsp **olive oil** in a large skillet over medium-high heat. Add 4 oz **shiitake mushrooms** (sliced) and 8 oz small **button mushrooms** (quartered). Season with ¼ tsp **salt** and cook, stirring often, until golden brown and tender, 10 to 12 minutes. Add 1 **red chili** (thinly sliced, or ¼ to ½ tsp **crushed red pepper flakes**) and cook, tossing, for 1 minute; stir in ½ cup **fresh flat-leaf parsley** (chopped). Add 2 cups **marinara** and simmer until heated through, about 3 minutes. Toss with 12 oz cooked **linguine** or other long pasta. Serve with grated **Parmesan**.

♥ **PER SERVING (WITH PASTA)** 492 CAL, 14 G FAT (2 G SAT FAT), 0 MG CHOL, 505 MG SOD, 16 G PRO, 78 G CAR, 6 G FIBER

### ④ *Italian sausage & spinach orecchiette*

**ACTIVE** 25 MIN • **TOTAL** 25 MIN • **SERVES** 4
COST PER SERVING $2.60

Heat 1 Tbsp **olive oil** in a large skillet over medium heat. Add 1 lb **Italian sausage** (casings removed) and cook, breaking it up with a spoon, until no longer pink, 5 to 7 minutes. Add 1 bunch **spinach** (thick stems discarded), season with ¼ tsp each **salt** and **pepper** and cook, tossing, for 1 minute. Add 2 cups **marinara** and simmer until heated through, about 3 minutes. Toss with 12 oz cooked **orecchiette** pasta or other short pasta. Serve with a dollop of **ricotta cheese**.

**PER SERVING (WITH PASTA)** 831 CAL, 44 G FAT (15 G SAT FAT), 91 MG CHOL, 1,396 MG SOD, 32 G PRO, 75 G CAR, 6 G FIBER

# Top this!

Ketchup, fine. Cheese, sure. But why not take your patties to a whole new place with surprising fixings.

START HERE

## BASIC BURGER

**ACTIVE** 15 MIN • **TOTAL** 15 MIN • **MAKES** 4

1¼  lb ground beef
     (85% lean)
     Kosher salt and
     pepper
4    hamburger buns

❶ Heat grill to medium-high. Gently form the beef into 4 balls. Don't overwork the meat—this can result in a tough, dry burger.

❷ Flatten each ball into a ¾-in.-thick patty. Make sure the top and sides are the same thickness throughout.

❸ Using your thumb, make a shallow 1½-in.-wide indent in the top of each patty (this will help the burgers maintain their shape while they cook). Season the patties with ½ tsp each salt and pepper.

❹ Lightly oil the grill. Place the patties on the grill, indent-side facing up, and cook until the burgers release easily from the grill, 4 to 5 minutes (don't press or flatten—this will dry them out). Flip and cook 4 to 5 minutes more for medium. Place on buns and top as desired.

## ❶ *Spicy Buffalo burger*

**ACTIVE** 15 MIN • **TOTAL** 15 MIN
**SERVES** 4 • COST PER SERVING $2.18

Prepare the burgers according to recipe directions. Meanwhile, whisk together 2 Tbsp **lowfat Greek yogurt**, 1 Tbsp **white wine vinegar** and ¼ tsp each **salt** and **pepper**. Add 3 stalks **celery** (thinly sliced), 2 oz crumbled **blue cheese** (½ cup), 1 **scallion** (chopped) and ¼ cup **fresh flat-leaf parsley** (chopped), and toss to combine. Top each burger with a piece of **iceberg lettuce**, 2 tsp **Buffalo wings sauce** and the **celery slaw**.

**PER BURGER** 371 CAL, 25.5 G FAT (11 G SAT FAT), 106 MG CHOL, 845 MG SOD, 31 G PRO, 3 G CAR, 1 G FIBER

## 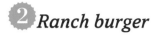 Ranch burger

**ACTIVE** 15 MIN • **TOTAL** 15 MIN • **SERVES** 4
COST PER SERVING $1.92

Prepare the burgers according to recipe directions. Top each with 1 Tbsp **ranch dressing**, 1 piece **green leaf lettuce**, 2 slices **tomato** and ¼ cup **plain potato chips**.

PER BURGER 434 CAL, 34 G FAT (10 G SAT FAT), 101 MG CHOL, 538 MG SOD, 37 G PRO, 7 G CAR, 1 G FIBER

## ③ South-of-the-border burger

**ACTIVE** 15 MIN • **TOTAL** 15 MIN • **SERVES** 4
COST PER SERVING $2.11

Prepare the burgers according to recipe directions, topping each burger with 1 thin slice of **Pepper Jack cheese** during the last 2 minutes of cooking. Top the burgers with ½ **avocado** (sliced) and ¾ cup **fresh salsa**.

PER BURGER 408 CAL, 29.5 G FAT (12.5 G SAT FAT), 111 MG CHOL, 503 MG SOD, 30 G PRO, 4 G CAR, 2 G FIBER

## ④ Reuben burger

**ACTIVE** 15 MIN • **TOTAL** 15 MIN • **SERVES** 4
COST PER SERVING $2.39

Prepare the burgers according to recipe directions, topping each burger with 1 thin slice of **Swiss cheese** during the last 2 minutes of cooking. Top each with 2 slices cooked **bacon** and ¼ cup prepared **coleslaw**.

PER BURGER 512 CAL, 36 G FAT (14 G SAT FAT), 131 MG CHOL, 958 MG SOD, 37 G PRO, 9 G CAR, 1 G FIBER

# Celebrate with ham

Take a baked ham, add a tasty glaze (sweet or savory) and—presto!—an easy, delicious dinner for a crowd.

## GLAZED HAM

**ACTIVE** 5 MIN • **TOTAL** 1 HR 25 MIN • **SERVES** 8 (WITH LEFTOVERS)

½   **fully cooked bone-in ham (about 7 lb total; preferably shank end)**

1   **glaze recipe (see recipes on the next page)**

❶ Heat oven to 375°F. Place the ham, cut-side down, on a rack set in a roasting pan; add ¼ cup water to the pan. score the ham, if desired. Cover the ham and the pan with foil and bake for 40 minutes.

❷ Brush half the glaze (not including any you have reserved) over the ham and continue baking, uncovered, for 20 minutes.

❸ Brush the other half of the glaze over the ham and bake until the internal temperature reaches 140°F, 15 to 20 minutes more. Serve with any reserved glaze.

## 1 Cranberry-ginger glazed ham

**ACTIVE** 10 MIN • **TOTAL** 10 MIN • **SERVES** 8 (WITH LEFTOVERS)
COST PER SERVING 2.39

In a small, heavy-bottomed saucepan, combine 1 cup **cranberry juice cocktail**, ¾ cup **dried cranberries**, ¼ cup **low-sodium soy sauce**, 2 tsp grated **fresh ginger** and 2 cloves **garlic** (finely chopped); bring to a boil. Transfer to a blender. Add 1 Tbsp **olive oil** and purée until smooth. Reserve ½ cup glaze for serving, then glaze the ham as directed.

PER SERVING (INCLUDES HAM) 243 CAL, 11 G FAT (4 G SAT FAT), 67 MG CHOL, 1,854 MG SOD, 26 G PRO, 8 G CAR, 0 G FIBER

## 2 Orange-coriander glazed ham

**ACTIVE** 5 MIN • **TOTAL** 5 MIN • **SERVES** 8 (WITH LEFTOVERS)
COST PER SERVING $1.19

Using a heavy pan, crush 3 Tbsp **coriander seeds** and 1½ tsp **black peppercorns**; place them in a bowl. (you can substitute 1½ tsp **ground coriander** for the seeds.) Add one 18-oz jar **orange marmalade** (about 1½ cups) and ¼ cup **white wine vinegar** and whisk to combine. Reserve ½ cup glaze for serving, then glaze the ham as directed.

PER SERVING (INCLUDES HAM) 294 CAL, 10 G FAT (4 G SAT FAT), 67 MG CHOL, 1,722 MG SOD, 26 G PRO, 25 G CAR, 0 G FIBER

## ③ *Balsamic-honey mustard glazed ham*

**ACTIVE** 5 MIN • **TOTAL** 5 MIN • **SERVES** 8 (WITH LEFTOVERS)
COST PER SERVING $1.31

Using a heavy pan, crush 2 tsp **black peppercorns**; place them in a bowl. Add ½ cup each **honey** and **whole-grain mustard** and ¼ cup each **Dijon mustard** and **balsamic vinegar** and whisk to combine. Reserve ½ cup glaze for serving, then glaze the ham as directed.

PER SERVING (INCLUDES HAM) 263 CAL, 11 G FAT (4 G SAT FAT), 67 MG CHOL, 1,925 MG SOD, 27 G PRO, 13 G CAR, 1 G FIBER

## ④ *Bourbon, molasses & spice glazed ham*

**ACTIVE** 5 MIN • **TOTAL** 20 MIN • **SERVES** 8 (WITH LEFTOVERS)
COST PER SERVING $1.22

In a small, heavy-bottomed saucepan, combine ½ cup each **bourbon** and **apple juice**, ¼ cup **molasses**, 2 Tbsp each **paprika** and packed **brown sugar**, 1 tsp **dry mustard**, and ½ tsp each **ground cinnamon** and **pepper**; bring to a boil. Reduce heat and simmer until the mixture is reduced by half and coats the back of a spoon, 12 to 15 minutes. Glaze the ham as directed.

PER SERVING (INCLUDES HAM) 239 CAL, 10 G FAT (4 G SAT FAT), 67 MG CHOL, 1,705 MG SOD, 26 G PRO, 8 G CAR, 0 G FIBER

# Mighty meatballs

On top of spaghetti...is just one delicious way to serve this dinnertime favorite.

START HERE

## BASIC MEATBALLS

**ACTIVE** 15 MIN • **TOTAL** 25 MIN • **SERVES** 4 • COST PER SERVING 65¢

- 1 large egg
  Kosher salt and pepper
- 1 clove garlic, finely chopped
- ½ cup fresh flat-leaf parsley, chopped
- ¼ cup bread crumbs
- 1 lb ground beef (85% lean)

Heat broiler. Line a rimmed baking sheet with nonstick foil. In a large bowl, whisk together the egg, 2 Tbsp water and ½ tsp each salt and pepper. Stir in the garlic and parsley, then the bread crumbs. Let sit for 2 minutes. Add the beef and mix to combine. Form the meat mixture into 1½-in. balls (about 20 total) and place on the prepared baking sheet. Broil until cooked through, 6 to 8 minutes.

PER SERVING 243 CAL, 14 G FAT (5 G SAT FAT), 116 MG CHOL, 373 MG SOD, 23 G PRO, 5 G CAR, 1 G FIBER

### 1 *Mexican meatballs*

**ACTIVE** 25 MIN • **TOTAL** 25 MIN
**SERVES** 4 • COST PER SERVING $1.36

Make the basic meatballs with the following changes: Substitute **ground pork** for the beef, **fresh cilantro** for the parsley and ¼ cup crushed **tortilla chips** (about 8; ¾ oz) for the bread crumbs. Add 1 Tbsp **paprika**, 1½ tsp **ground cumin** and 1 tsp **dried oregano** along with the salt and pepper. Cook as directed. In a large skillet, combine 2 cups **marinara sauce**, 1 Tbsp **chopped chipotle in adobo** plus 2 tsp **adobo sauce** and ¼ tsp **ground cinnamon** and bring to a simmer. Add the cooked meatballs and toss to coat. Serve over steamed white rice and top with fresh cilantro and sour cream, if desired.

PER SERVING 549 CAL, 22 G FAT (7 G SAT FAT), 125 MG CHOL, 947 MG SOD, 29 G PRO, 51 G CAR, 5 G FIBER

## ② *Gingery meatball soup with bok choy*

**ACTIVE** 25 MIN • **TOTAL** 30 MIN • **SERVES** 4
COST PER SERVING $2.25

Make the basic meatballs with the following changes: Substitute **ground chicken** for the beef and **fresh cilantro** for the parsley. Add 2 **scallions** (finely chopped) and 1 Tbsp grated **fresh ginger** along with the salt and pepper. Cook as directed. In a large saucepan, bring 6 cups **low-sodium chicken broth** and one 2-in. piece **fresh ginger** and **red chili** (each thinly sliced) to a boil. Add 1 medium **carrot** (thinly sliced) and simmer for 1 minute. Add 4 heads **baby bok choy** (about 12 oz, trimmed; leaves separated) and simmer until just tender, about 2 minutes. Gently stir in the cooked meatballs.

PER SERVING 294 CAL, 13 G FAT (4 G SAT FAT), 138 MG CHOL, 545 MG SOD, 32 G PRO, 13 G CAR, 3 G FIBER

## ③ *Turkey meatball stroganoff*

**ACTIVE** 30 MIN • **TOTAL** 30 MIN • **SERVES** 4
COST PER SERVING $2.83

Make the basic meatballs with the following changes: Substitute **ground turkey** for the beef and **red currant jelly** for the water. Add $\frac{1}{8}$ tsp **ground allspice** along with the salt and pepper. Cook as directed. Heat 2 Tbsp **olive oil** in a large skillet over medium-high heat. Add a 10-oz package **cremini or white mushrooms** (sliced), season with $\frac{1}{4}$ tsp each **salt** and **pepper** and cook, tossing occasionally, until golden brown and tender, 4 to 5 minutes. Add $\frac{3}{4}$ cup **dry white wine** and simmer for 1 minute. Remove from heat; stir in $\frac{1}{3}$ cup **lowfat sour cream** and 1 Tbsp **Dijon mustard** and toss with the cooked meatballs. Top with chopped fresh flat-leaf parsley and serve over egg noodles.

PER SERVING 665 CAL, 22 G FAT (5 G SAT FAT), 212 MG CHOL, 645 MG SOD, 40 G PRO, 79 G CAR, 3 G FIBER

## ④ *Meatball calzones with broccoli rabe & provolone*

**ACTIVE** 30 MIN • **TOTAL** 30 MIN • **SERVES** 4
COST PER SERVING $2.07

Make the basic meatballs with the following changes: Substitute 8 oz **Italian sausage** for half the beef. Cook as directed. Cook $\frac{1}{2}$ bunch **broccoli rabe** (trimmed) in boiling water until just tender, about 3 minutes. Drain, squeezing out excess water; roughly chop. Heat oven to 425°F. On a lightly floured surface, shape 1 lb **pizza dough** (at room temperature) into four 8-in. rounds. Dividing evenly, top half of each round with the cooked meatballs, broccoli rabe, $\frac{1}{4}$ cup **sweet red cherry peppers** (such as Peppadews; chopped) and 4 oz **provolone** (coarsely grated). Fold the dough over the filling and pinch the edges to seal; place on a parchment-lined baking sheet. Lightly brush the tops with **olive oil** and bake until golden brown, 20 to 25 minutes. Serve with warmed marinara sauce for dipping, if desired.

PER SERVING 668 CAL, 29 G FAT (11 G SAT FAT), 120 MG CHOL, 1,806 MG SOD, 34 G PRO, 61 G CAR, 3 G FIBER

# Razzle-dazzle risotto

No longer a mere side dish, these creamy rice creations will stand out as the main event.

**START HERE**

## BASIC CREAMY RISOTTO

**ACTIVE** 15 MIN • **TOTAL** 40 MIN • **SERVES** 4 • **COST PER SERVING** $1.38

2 Tbsp olive oil

1 medium onion, finely chopped

  Kosher salt and pepper

2 cloves garlic, finely chopped

¾ cup Arborio rice

¾ cup dry white wine

3½ cups low-sodium chicken or vegetable broth

¼ cup grated Romano or Parmesan (1 oz), plus more for serving

❶ Heat the oil in a large skillet over medium heat. Add the onion, ½ tsp salt and ¼ tsp pepper and cook, covered, stirring occasionally, until tender, 6 to 8 minutes. Add the garlic and cook, stirring, for 1 minute.

❷ Add the rice and cook, stirring, for 1 minute. Add the wine and simmer until absorbed, 5 to 7 minutes.

❸ Add the broth and simmer, stirring occasionally, until the rice is tender and creamy and the broth has been absorbed, 18 to 20 minutes; stir in the Romano cheese. Serve with additional Romano, if desired.

♥ **PER SERVING** 267 CAL, 11 G FAT (3 G SAT FAT), 10 MG CHOL, 439 MG SOD, 10 G PRO, 33 G CAR, 1 G FIBER

 ***Chicken sausage, green bean & tomato risotto***

**ACTIVE** 25 MIN • **TOTAL** 40 MIN
**SERVES** 4 • **COST PER SERVING** $2.34

Prepare the risotto. Meanwhile, heat 1 Tbsp **olive oil** in a large skillet over medium-high heat. Add 8 oz **fully cooked chicken sausage** (sliced) and cook until browned, about 3 minutes. Add 4 oz **green beans** (thinly sliced) and cook until heated through, about 3 minutes; toss with 3 **plum tomatoes** (seeded and chopped). Fold the sausage mixture into the risotto along with ½ cup **fresh cilantro** (roughly chopped).

**PER SERVING** 409 CAL, 19 G FAT (5 G SAT FAT), 54 MG CHOL, 950 MG SOD, 20 G PRO, 38 G CAR, 3 G FIBER

### 3 *Spring pea & scallion risotto*

**ACTIVE** 20 MIN • **TOTAL** 40 MIN
**SERVES** 4 • COST PER SERVING $1.99

Prepare the risotto. Stir in 4 oz **snow peas** (sliced crosswise) and ½ cup **frozen peas** (thawed); cook until heated through, about 3 minutes. Fold in 2 **scallions** (thinly sliced).

♥ **PER SERVING** 292 CAL, 11 G FAT (3 G SAT FAT), 10 MG CHOL, 440 MG SOD, 12 G PRO, 38 G CAR, 3 G FIBER

### 2 *Mushroom & herb risotto*

**ACTIVE** 25 MIN • **TOTAL** 40 MIN • **SERVES** 4
COST PER SERVING $2.27

Prepare the risotto. Meanwhile, heat 2 Tbsp **olive oil** in a large skillet over medium-high heat. Add 12 oz small **button mushrooms** (quartered), season with ¼ tsp each **salt** and **pepper** and cook, tossing occasionally, until golden brown and tender, 5 to 6 minutes. Fold in ½ cup **fresh flat-leaf parsley** (chopped) and 1 Tbsp **fresh tarragon** (chopped). Fold the mushroom mixture into the risotto.

♥ **PER SERVING** 350 CAL, 18 G FAT (4 G SAT FAT), 10 MG CHOL, 568 MG SOD, 13 G PRO, 37 G CAR, 2 G FIBER

*Shrimp, lemon & basil risotto*

**ACTIVE** 25 MIN • **TOTAL** 40 MIN • **SERVES** 4
COST PER SERVING $3.48

Prepare the risotto. Meanwhile, using a vegetable peeler, remove 3 strips of **zest** from 1 **lemon** then thinly slice the zest. Heat 1 Tbsp **olive oil** in a large skillet over medium-high heat. Season 1 lb **medium peeled and deveined shrimp** with ½ tsp **salt** and cook for 2 minutes. Turn the shrimp, add the lemon zest and 3 Tbsp **fresh lemon juice** and cook until the shrimp are opaque throughout, 1 to 2 minutes more. Fold the shrimp mixture into the risotto along with ½ cup **fresh basil** (torn).

PER SERVING 392 CAL, 14 G FAT (3 G SAT FAT), 130 MG CHOL, 891 MG SOD, 29 G PRO, 35 G CAR, 2 G FIBER

# Hot off the grill

## Top tonight's sausages with easy-to-make relishes.

**START HERE**

### PERFECTLY COOKED ITALIAN SAUSAGES

**ACTIVE** 15 MIN • **TOTAL** 15 MIN • **SERVES** 4

- **4** large sweet or hot Italian sausage links (about 1½ lb total)
- **1** Tbsp olive oil

Heat a grill, grill pan or skillet to medium-high heat. Coat the sausages with the oil and cook, covered, turning occasionally, until just cooked through, 12 to 15 minutes.

### ❶ *Sausages with pickled red onion & jalapeño relish*

**ACTIVE** 20 MIN • **TOTAL** 25 MIN
**SERVES** 4
COST PER SERVING $1.81

In a bowl, whisk together 2 Tbsp **fresh lime juice**, 1 Tbsp **olive oil**, ½ tsp **honey** and a pinch each **salt** and **pepper**. Add 2 **jalapeños** (seeded and thinly sliced), ½ small **red onion** (finely chopped) and ¼ cup **fresh cilantro** (roughly chopped). Let sit, tossing occasionally, for 15 minutes. Meanwhile, cook the sausages as directed. Serve the sausages in 4 rolls and top with the relish.

PER SERVING 600 CAL, 35 G FAT (11 G SAT FAT), 49 MG CHOL, 1,472 MG SOD, 25 G PRO, 47 G CAR, 3 G FIBER

## 2 Sausages with white bean & cherry pepper relish

**ACTIVE** 20 MIN • **TOTAL** 20 MIN
**SERVES** 4
**COST PER SERVING** $1.94

Cook the sausages as directed. In a bowl, combine half a 15.5-oz can **small white beans** (rinsed), 4 **sweet red cherry peppers** (such as Peppadew; thinly sliced), 2 **scallions** (thinly sliced), 1 small **carrot** (thinly sliced into half-moons), 1 Tbsp each **olive oil** and **white wine vinegar** and a pinch each **salt** and **pepper**. Serve the sausages in 4 rolls and top with the relish.

**PER SERVING** 668 CAL, 35 G FAT (11 G SAT FAT), 49 MG CHOL, 1,770 MG SOD, 29 G PRO, 60 G CAR, 6 G FIBER

### 3 Sausages with creamy apple & celery relish

**ACTIVE** 15 MIN • **TOTAL** 20 MIN • **SERVES** 4
COST PER SERVING $1.77

Cook the sausages as directed. In a bowl, whisk together 1 Tbsp **mayonnaise**, 1 tsp each **whole-grain mustard** and **lemon zest**, 1 Tbsp **fresh lemon juice** and a pinch each **salt** and **pepper**. Toss with 1 stalk **celery** (thinly sliced), ½ **Granny Smith apple** (cut into thin ½-in. pieces) and ¼ cup **fresh flat-leaf parsley** (roughly chopped). Serve the sausages in 4 rolls and top with the relish.

PER SERVING 603 CAL, 35 G FAT (11 G SAT FAT), 49 MG CHOL, 1,527 MG SOD, 26 G PRO, 49 G CAR, 4 G FIBER

### 4 Sausages with balsamic tomatoes & blue cheese relish

**ACTIVE** 20 MIN • **TOTAL** 20 MIN • **SERVES** 4
COST PER SERVING $1.95

Cook the sausages as directed. In a bowl, whisk together 2 Tbsp **olive oil**, 1 Tbsp **balsamic vinegar** and a pinch each **salt** and **pepper**. Toss with 1 cup **grape tomatoes** (sliced) and ½ small **red onion** (thinly sliced). Fold in 1 cup **spinach** (roughly chopped) and 1 oz **blue cheese** (crumbled). Serve the sausages in 4 rolls and top with the relish.

PER SERVING 658 CAL, 40 G FAT (13 G SAT FAT), 55 MG CHOL, 1,578 MG SOD, 27 G PRO, 47 G CAR, 3 G FIBER

### 5 Sausages with orange, olive & sweet onion relish

**ACTIVE** 20 MIN • **TOTAL** 20 MIN
**SERVES** 4 • COST PER SERVING $1.98

Cook the sausages as directed. Cut away the peel and white pith of 2 **oranges**. Working over a bowl, cut the oranges into segments. Cut the segments into ½-in. pieces. Add ¼ **sweet onion** (finely chopped), ¼ cup each small **pitted green olives** (quartered) and **fresh flat-leaf parsley** (roughly chopped) to the bowl. Gently toss with 1 Tbsp **olive oil** and a pinch each **salt** and **pepper**. Serve the sausages in 4 rolls and top with the relish.

PER SERVING 643 CAL, 36 G FAT (11 G SAT FAT), 49 MG CHOL, 1,592 MG SOD, 26 G PRO, 55 G CAR, 5 G FIBER

# Crispy chicken cutlets

Turn this dinner staple into a standout dish with four surprising variations.

**START HERE**

## BASIC CHICKEN CUTLETS

**ACTIVE** 15 MIN • **TOTAL** 15 • **SERVES** 4 • **COST PER SERVING** $1.08

- 8 small chicken cutlets (about 1½ lb total)
- Kosher salt and pepper
- 1 cup panko bread crumbs
- ¼ cup olive oil

**1** Season the chicken with ¾ tsp salt and ¼ tsp pepper. Coat the cutlets in the bread crumbs, pressing gently to help them adhere.

**2** Heat 2 Tbsp oil in a large skillet over medium-high heat. Add half the cutlets and cook until golden brown and cooked through, 2 to 3 minutes per side; transfer to a plate and wipe out the skillet. Repeat with the remaining oil and cutlets.

**PER SERVING** 369 CAL, 16 G FAT (3 G SAT FAT), 94 MG CHOL, 487 MG SOD, 36 G PRO, 17 G CAR, 0 G FIBER

## 1 *Chicken & spinach Parmesan*

**ACTIVE** 5 MIN • **TOTAL** 10 MIN (PLUS COOKING THE CUTLETS)
**SERVES** 4
**COST PER SERVING** $1.21

Spread 2 Tbsp **marinara** sauce on the bottom of 4 small casserole dishes and top each with 2 cooked **cutlets**. Top each with ½ cup **baby spinach** (chopped), 2 Tbsp **marinara** and 2 Tbsp grated **mozzarella** (or use one large baking dish and multiply the ingredients by 4). Broil until the cheese begins to brown, 2 to 3 minutes.

**PER SERVING** 471 CAL, 21 G FAT (5 G SAT FAT), 106 MG CHOL, 857 MG SOD, 41 G PRO, 27 G CAR, 2 G FIBER

### 3 Chicken cutlets with ham & Swiss cheese

**ACTIVE** 5 MIN • **TOTAL** 10 MIN (PLUS COOKING THE CUTLETS) • **SERVES** 4
COST PER SERVING $1.33

Place the cooked **cutlets** on a foil-lined, broiler-proof baking sheet. Spread ½ tsp **Dijon mustard** on each cutlet. Top each with a thin slice of **deli ham** and **Swiss cheese**. Sprinkle with 2 tsp **fresh thyme** and broil until the cheese begins to brown, 2 to 3 minutes. Serve with salad, if desired.

PER SERVING 605 CAL, 31 G FAT (10 G SAT FAT), 166 MG CHOL, 1,418 MG SOD, 55 G PRO, 20 G CAR, 1 G FIBER

### 2 Chicken cutlets with sautéed bell peppers & feta cheese

**ACTIVE** 10 MIN • **TOTAL** 10 MIN (PLUS COOKING THE CUTLETS)
**SERVES** 4 • COST PER SERVING $1.86

Heat 2 Tbsp **olive oil** in a large skillet over medium heat. Add 3 **bell peppers** (cut into ½-in. pieces), 2 Tbsp **raisins** and ¼ tsp each **salt** and **pepper** and cook, covered, stirring occasionally until very tender, 6 to 8 minutes. Add 2 cloves **garlic** (thinly sliced) and cook for 1 minute. Stir in 2 **scallions** (thinly sliced) and 1 Tbsp **red wine vinegar**. Serve the pepper mixture over the cooked **cutlets** and sprinkle with ¼ cup crumbled **feta**.

PER SERVING 503 CAL, 25 G FAT (5 G SAT FAT), 102 MG CHOL, 742 MG SOD, 39 G PRO, 29 G CAR, 2 G FIBER

### ④ *Chicken cutlets with oranges & chutney*

**ACTIVE** 10 MIN • **TOTAL** 10 MIN (PLUS COOKING THE CUTLETS)
**SERVES** 4 • COST PER SERVING $1.62

Heat 2 Tbsp **olive oil** in a medium skillet over medium heat. Add 2 cloves **garlic** (thinly sliced) and cook, stirring, until golden brown. Add 1 Tbsp **curry powder** and cook, stirring for 30 seconds. Add ¼ cup **Major Grey's chutney** and ¼ cup **orange juice** and cook until melted. Segment 1 **orange** and gently stir it into the chutney mixture. Serve the orange mixture over the cooked **cutlets** and **steamed rice** and sprinkle with chopped **cilantro**.

**PER SERVING** 505 CAL, 23 G FAT (3 G SAT FAT), 94 MG CHOL, 739 MG SOD, 37 G PRO, 35 G CAR, 1 G FIBER

# Taming the flame

Take dinner outdoors with juicy kebabs that cook up fast and are full of flavor.

## FOR ALL KEBABS

Heat grill to medium-high. In a large bowl, toss ingredients with 2 Tbsp **olive oil** and ½ tsp each **salt** and **pepper**. Thread onto skewers and grill as directed.

###  Italian sausage & grape kebabs

**ACTIVE** 20 MIN • **TOTAL** 20 MIN • **SERVES** 4 • **COST PER SERVING** $1.63

Heat the grill, toss 1½ lb **sweet Italian sausage** links (cut crosswise into 1½-in. pieces) and 1 cup **large seedless red grapes** in the olive oil, salt and pepper and thread onto skewers. Grill, turning occasionally, until the sausages are cooked through, 10 to 12 minutes.

PER SERVING 385 CAL, 31 G FAT (9 G SAT FAT), 49 MG CHOL, 1,289 MG SOD, 17 G PRO, 11 G CAR, 1 G FIBER

###  Chicken, pineapple & red pepper kebabs

**ACTIVE** 20 MIN • **TOTAL** 20 MIN • **SERVES** 4 • **COST PER SERVING** $1.28

Heat the grill, toss 1½ lb **boneless, skinless chicken breasts** (cut into 1½-in. pieces), 1 **red pepper** (cut into 1-in. pieces) and 8 oz **fresh pineapple** (cut into 1-in. chunks) with the olive oil, salt and pepper and thread onto skewers. Grill, turning occasionally, until the chicken is cooked through, 8 to 10 minutes.

♥ PER SERVING 295 CAL, 11 G FAT (2 G SAT FAT), 36 MG CHOL, 280 MG SOD, 14 G PRO, 5 G CAR, 2 G FIBER

###  Salmon & scallion kebabs

**ACTIVE** 15 MIN • **TOTAL** 15 MIN • **SERVES** 4 • **COST PER SERVING** $1.01

Heat the grill, toss ½ lb **skinless salmon fillet** (cut into 1½-in. pieces) and 2 bunches **scallions** (white and light green parts only; cut into 1½-in. pieces) in the olive oil, salt and pepper and thread onto skewers. Grill, turning occasionally, until the salmon is opaque throughout, 4 to 6 minutes.

♥ PER SERVING 174 CAL, 11 G FAT (2 G SAT FAT), 36 MG CHOL, 280 MG SOD, 14 G PRO, 5 G CAR, 2 G FIBER

## 4 *Beef, orange & broccoli kebabs*

**ACTIVE** 20 MIN • **TOTAL** 20 MIN • **SERVES** 4
COST PER SERVING $3.37

Heat the grill, toss 1½ lb **sirloin steak** (cut into 1½-in. pieces), 1 small head **broccoli** (cut into medium florets) and 1 **navel orange** (cut into 1-in. pieces) with the oil and salt and pepper and thread onto skewers. Grill, turning occasionally, to desired doneness, 8 to 10 minutes for medium-rare.

**PER SERVING** 363 CAL, 19 G FAT (6 G SAT FAT), 112 MG CHOL, 334 MG SOD, 39 G PRO, 7 G CAR, 2 G FIBER

## 5 *Shrimp, zucchini & tomato kebabs*

**ACTIVE** 15 MIN • **TOTAL** 15 MIN • **SERVES** 4
COST PER SERVING $2.01

Heat the grill, toss ¾ lb **large peeled and deveined shrimp**, 2 small **zucchini** (cut into ¼-in. half-moons), 1 cup **grape tomatoes** with the oil and salt and pepper and thread onto skewers. Grill, turning occasionally, until the shrimp are opaque throughout, 4 to 5 minutes.

♥ **PER SERVING** 117 CAL, 8 G FAT (1 G SAT FAT), 71 MG CHOL, 569 MG SOD, 9 G PRO, 4 G CAR, 1 G FIBER

## 6 *Pork, yellow pepper & jalapeño kebabs*

**ACTIVE** 20 MIN • **TOTAL** 20 MIN • **SERVES** 4
COST PER SERVING $1.11

Heat the grill, toss 1½ lb **pork loin** (cut into 1½-in. pieces), 4 **jalapeños** (cut into ½-in. pieces), 1 **yellow pepper** (cut into 1-in. pieces) with the olive oil, salt and pepper and thread onto skewers. Grill, turning occasionally, until the pork is just cooked through, 8 to 10 minutes. During the last 3 minutes of grilling, baste with a mixture of ½ cup **apricot jam** and 2 Tbsp **white wine vinegar**.

**PER SERVING** 404 CAL, 27 G FAT (8 G SAT FAT), 105 MG CHOL, 321 MG SOD, 36 G PRO, 3 G CAR, 1 G FIBER

## 7 *Chicken & green bean kebabs*

**ACTIVE** 20 MIN • **TOTAL** 20 MIN • **SERVES** 4
COST PER SERVING $1.68

Heat the grill, toss 1½ lb **boneless, skinless chicken breasts** (cut into 1½-in. pieces) and 8 oz **green beans** (cut into 2-in. pieces) with the oil and salt and pepper and thread onto skewers. Dust threaded skewers with ½ tsp **Cajun seasoning** (no salt added) and grill, turning occasionally, until the chicken is cooked through, 8 to 10 minutes.

♥ **PER SERVING** 260 CAL, 11 G FAT (2 G SAT FAT), 94 MG CHOL, 326 MG SOD, 35 G PRO, 4 G CAR, 2 G FIBER

# Pizza party

Shape your dough like a pro,
then top it off with exciting flavor
combos that really deliver.

START HERE

### PREPARING PIZZA DOUGH

**1** Thaw 1 lb store-bought pizza dough (if frozen). Let sit at room temperature for 30 minutes.

**2** Using floured fingertips, transfer the dough to a lightly floured surface and gently shape into a small, flat disk.

**3** Working from the center of the disk, spread fingers to push the dough outward to create a larger circle.

**4** Lift the dough and move your hands along the edges, allowing gravity to pull and stretch the dough into a 16-in. oval, circle or rectangle.

**5** Heat oven to 425°F and dust a baking sheet with cornmeal. Place the shaped dough on the prepared baking sheet, top as desired and bake until golden brown and crisp, 20 to 25 minutes.

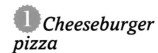

## **1** *Cheeseburger pizza*

**ACTIVE** 15 MIN • **TOTAL** 40 MIN
**SERVES** 4 • COST PER SERVING $1.59

Heat the oven and prepare the pizza dough as directed. Heat a large skillet over medium heat. Add 8 oz **lean ground beef**; cook, breaking it up with a spoon, until no longer pink, about 5 minutes. Remove from heat and stir in ½ cup **barbecue sauce**. Spoon the mixture over the prepared dough and sprinkle with 2 oz **extra-sharp Cheddar** (grated; ½ cup). Bake as directed. In a large bowl, toss together 1 head **butter**, **Bibb** or **Boston lettuce** (torn), ½ pint **cherry tomatoes** (quartered), ½ small **red onion** (thinly sliced), 1 Tbsp **olive oil** and ¼ tsp each **salt** and **pepper**. Top pizza with salad and serve immediately.

**PER SERVING** 532 CAL, 16 G FAT (6 G SAT FAT), 52 MG CHOL, 1,095 MG SOD, 26 G PRO, 68 G CAR, 1 G FIBER

## ② *Bacon, corn & poblano pizza*

**ACTIVE** 15 MIN • **TOTAL** 40 MIN • **SERVES** 4
COST PER SERVING $1.07

Heat the oven and prepare the pizza dough as directed. Cut 6 slices **bacon** into 1-in. pieces. Cook the bacon in a medium skillet over medium heat, stirring occasionally, for 4 minutes. Transfer to a paper towel–lined plate. In a large bowl, toss together 1 cup fresh **corn kernels** (from 1 to 2 ears), 1 large **poblano** or **green pepper** (seeded and thinly sliced), 3 **scallions** (thinly sliced), 1 Tbsp **olive oil** and ¼ tsp each **salt** and **pepper**. Fold in 3 oz **Monterey Jack cheese** (grated; ¾ cup) and the bacon. Scatter the mixture over the dough and bake as directed.

PER SERVING 501 CAL, 18 G FAT (6 G SAT FAT), 32 MG CHOL, 1,098 MG SOD, 22 G PRO, 65 G CAR, 1 G FIBER

## ③ *Salami, spinach & provolone pizza*

**ACTIVE** 10 MIN • **TOTAL** 35 MIN • **SERVES** 4
COST PER SERVING $1.28

Heat the oven and prepare the pizza dough as directed. Arrange 1 bunch **spinach** (thick stems discarded; large leaves torn), ¼ lb thinly sliced **provolone** and 2 oz thinly sliced **hard salami** over the dough. Scatter 2 **pepperoncini peppers** (thinly sliced) over the top and bake as directed.

PER SERVING 449 CAL, 14 G FAT (6 G SAT FAT), 34 MG CHOL, 1,317 MG SOD, 23 G, PRO, 58 G CAR, 2 G FIBER

## ④ *Lasagna pizza*

**ACTIVE** 10 MIN • **TOTAL** 35 MIN • **SERVES** 4
COST PER SERVING $1.63

Heat the oven and prepare the pizza dough as directed. In a medium bowl, combine ¾ cup **part-skim ricotta**, 2 cloves **garlic** (finely chopped), 1 oz **Parmesan** (grated; ¼ cup) and ½ tsp each **salt** and **pepper**. Fold in ½ cup each **fresh flat-leaf parsley** and **fresh basil** (chopped) and 1 oz **mozzarella** (grated; ¼ cup). Spread ¾ cup **marinara sauce** over the dough; dollop the ricotta mixture over the top. Sprinkle with 2 oz **mozzarella** (grated; ½ cup) and bake as directed.

PER SERVING 474 CAL, 12 G FAT (5 G SAT FAT), 20 MG CHOL, 1,245 MG SOD, 24 G PRO, 65 G CAR, 2 G FIBER

## ⑤ *Lemony zucchini, fresh garlic & Parmesan pizza*

**ACTIVE** 10 MIN • **TOTAL** 35 MIN • **SERVES** 4
COST PER SERVING $1.07

Heat the oven and prepare the pizza dough as directed. Using a vegetable peeler, remove 3 strips of **zest** from a **lemon**; thinly slice the zest. In a large bowl, toss together the zest, 3 medium **zucchini** (about 1 lb; thinly sliced) and 2 large cloves **garlic** (thinly sliced) with 2 Tbsp each **olive oil** and grated **Parmesan**, ¼ to ½ tsp **crushed red pepper flakes** and ½ tsp **salt**. Scatter the mixture over the dough; sprinkle with 2 Tbsp grated **Parmesan**. Bake as directed.

PER SERVING 379 CAL, 10 G FAT (2 G SAT FAT), 4 MG CHOL, 899 MG SOD, 14 G PRO, 58 G CAR, 2 G FIBER

# Easy cheesy shells

Shake up this family classic with new flavors, from creamy chicken to zesty shrimp.

START HERE

## BASIC THREE-CHEESE STUFFED SHELLS

**ACTIVE** 15 MIN • **TOTAL** 35 MIN • **SERVES** 4 • **COST PER SERVING** $2.47

| | |
|---|---|
| 16 | jumbo shells (from a 12-oz box) |
| 1¾ | cups marinara sauce or béchamel (recipe below) |
| 1 | 15-oz container ricotta |
| 4 | cups baby spinach, roughly chopped |
| ¾ | cup fresh flat-leaf parsley, basil or a combination, chopped |
| 2 | oz Parmesan or Romano, grated (about ½ cup) |
| 4 | oz part-skim mozzarella, coarsely grated (about 1 cup) |
| | Kosher salt and pepper |

❶ Heat oven to 400°F. Cook the shells according to package directions. Drain and rinse under cold water to cool.
❷ Spread the marinara or béchamel sauce on the bottom of a large broiler-proof baking dish.
❸ In a large bowl, combine the ricotta, spinach, herbs, Parmesan, ½ cup mozzarella and ½ tsp each salt and pepper. Spoon the mixture into the shells (about ¼ cup per shell) and place on top of the sauce.
❹ Sprinkle with the remaining ½ cup mozzarella, cover with foil and bake until the shells are heated through, 12 to 15 minutes. Heat broiler. Uncover, and broil until the cheese begins to brown, 2 to 3 minutes.

**PER SERVING** 558 CAL, 26 G FAT (15 G SAT FAT), 84 MG CHOL, 1,262 MG SOD, 33 G PRO, 49 G CAR, 5 G FIBER

## BASIC BÉCHAMEL

**ACTIVE** 5 MIN • **TOTAL** 20 MIN • **MAKES** 1¾ CUPS

In a small saucepan, combine 2 cups **whole milk**, ½ medium **onion**, 3 large cloves **garlic** (smashed) and 10 **peppercorns** and bring to a boil, stirring occasionally; remove from the heat. Melt 3 Tbsp **unsalted butter** in a medium saucepan over medium-low heat. Stir in 2 Tbsp **all-purpose flour**. Increase the heat to medium and cook, stirring, until the mixture is light golden brown, 3 to 5 minutes. Strain the milk, discarding the solids and gradually whisk it into the flour mixture (about ¾ cup at a time) until smooth. Simmer, stirring often, until thickened, 6 to 8 minutes. Remove from the heat and season with ¼ tsp each **salt** and **pepper**.

## ① *Sweet pea & mint shells*

**ACTIVE** 15 MIN • **TOTAL** 35 MIN • **SERVES** 4 • COST PER SERVING $2.10

Prepare the shells according to recipe instructions. Omit the filling. Prepare the **béchamel** and spread on the bottom of the baking dish. In a large bowl, combine a 15-oz container **ricotta cheese**, 3 **scallions** (finely chopped), ¾ cup grated **Romano cheese**, ¼ cup grated **mozzarella**, 1½ tsp finely grated **lemon zest** and ½ tsp each **salt** and **pepper**. Fold in 1½ cup **frozen peas** (thawed) and ½ cup each **fresh mint** and **fresh flat-leaf parsley** (roughly chopped). Spoon the mixture into the shells (about ¼ cup per shell), place on top of the sauce and sprinkle with ½ cup grated **mozzarella**. Bake and broil according to recipe directions.

**PER SERVING** 703 CAL, 38 G FAT (24 G SAT FAT), 136 MG CHOL, 1,059 MG SOD, 36 G PRO, 54 G CAR, 6 G FIBER

## ② *Chipotle beef & Cheddar shells*

**ACTIVE** 20 MIN • **TOTAL** 45 MIN • **SERVES** 4 • COST PER SERVING $2.82

Prepare the shells according to recipe instructions. Omit the filling. Combine 1¾ cups **marinara sauce** with 2 Tbsp **chipotle in adobo** (finely chopped) and spread on the bottom of the baking dish. Heat 1 Tbsp **olive oil** in a large skillet over medium heat. Sauté 1 **onion** (finely chopped) until very tender, 10 to 12 minutes. Stir in 1 clove **garlic** (finely chopped) and cook for 1 minute. Increase the heat to medium-high, add ¾ lb **lean ground beef** and cook, breaking it up with a spoon, until browned, 3 to 4 minutes. Stir in a 15-oz can **petite diced tomatoes with green chiles** (drained), 1 tsp **ground cumin** and ¼ tsp **ground cinnamon** and cook for 3 minutes. Remove from heat and fold in 1 cup **fresh cilantro** (chopped) and ½ cup grated **sharp Cheddar**. Spoon the mixture into the shells (about ¼ cup each) and place on top of the sauce. Sprinkle with ½ cup grated **sharp Cheddar** and bake and broil according to recipe directions. Squeeze 2 Tbsp **fresh lime juice** over the shells and serve with additional chopped cilantro and lime wedges, if desired.

**PER SERVING** 586 CAL, 27 G FAT (13 G SAT FAT), 108 MG CHOL, 971 MG SOD, 36 G PRO, 51 G CAR, 2 G FIBER

### ③ *Cheesy chicken & ham shells*

**ACTIVE** 35 MIN • **TOTAL** 55 MIN • **SERVES** 4 • COST PER SERVING $2.72

Prepare the shells according to recipe instructions. Omit the filling. Prepare the **béchamel** and spread all but ½ cup of the sauce on the bottom of the baking dish. In a large bowl, whisk together the ½ cup béchamel with 2 Tbsp **Dijon mustard** and 1 tsp **Worcestershire sauce**. Toss with 3 cups shredded **rotisserie chicken**. Fold in ¾ cup grated **Gruyère**, 2 oz thinly sliced **deli ham** (cut into ½-in. pieces), ½ small **red onion** (finely chopped), 1 Tbsp **fresh tarragon** (chopped) and ½ tsp **pepper**. Spoon the mixture into the shells (about ¼ cup each) and place on top of the sauce. In a bowl, combine ½ cup **panko bread crumbs** and 1½ Tbsp **olive oil**. Sprinkle over the shells and bake and broil according to recipe instructions.

PER SERVING 586 CAL, 27 G FAT (13 G SAT FAT), 108 MG CHOL, 971 MG SOD, 36 G PRO, 51 G CAR, 2 G FIBER

### ④ *Garlicky shrimp & feta shells*

**ACTIVE** 20 MIN • **TOTAL** 40 MIN • **SERVES** 4 • COST PER SERVING $3.05

Prepare the shells according to recipe instructions. Omit the filling. Spread 1¾ cups **marinara sauce** on the bottom of the baking dish. Remove 3 strips of **zest** from 1 **lemon**; thinly slice the zest. In a large skillet, heat 2 Tbsp **olive oil**, 2 large cloves **garlic** (finely chopped), the zest and ½ tsp **crushed red pepper flakes** over medium heat until the garlic begins to brown, about 2 minutes. Add 2 Tbsp each **fresh lemon juice** and **capers** (roughly chopped) and 1 **roasted red pepper** (cut into ¼-in. pieces) and toss to combine. Remove from the heat and stir in ½ cup **marinara sauce**. Toss with 12 oz **large peeled and deveined shrimp** (quartered) to coat. Fold in 2 cups **baby spinach** and ½ cup **fresh basil** (each roughly chopped), ¼ cup crumbled **feta** and ½ tsp each **salt** and **pepper**. Spoon the mixture into the shells and place on top of the sauce. Sprinkle with ¼ cup crumbled **feta** and bake and broil according to recipe directions.

PER SERVING 391 CAL, 13 G FAT (3.5 G SAT FAT), 122 MG CHOL, 1,550 MG SOD, 22 G PRO, 47 G CAR, 5 G FIBER

# Turkey time

## Just a few simple tweaks amp up the flavor of the Thanksgiving table's star player.

### BASIC HERB ROASTED TURKEY

**ACTIVE** 20 MIN • **TOTAL** 3 HR 45 MIN • **SERVES** 8 (WITH LEFTOVERS) • COST PER SERVING $3.65

1   12- to 14-lb turkey, thawed if frozen

8   sprigs fresh herbs, such as thyme, rosemary, sage or a combination, plus more for serving

3   medium onions, cut into wedges

2   Tbsp olive oil or melted butter

    Kosher salt

2   medium carrots, cut into 2-in. pieces

2   stalks celery, cut into 2-in. pieces

¾   cup low-sodium chicken broth

① Heat oven to 375°F. Remove the giblets and neck from the cavity. Using paper towels, pat the turkey dry. Stuff the herbs and half the onions into the main cavity.

② Tie the legs together with kitchen twine. Tuck the wing tips underneath the body. Rub the turkey with the oil and sprinkle with 2 tsp salt.

③ Place the turkey neck, carrots, celery and the remaining onions in a large roasting pan. Place a roasting rack in the pan and put the turkey on top of it.

④ Roast the turkey until a thermometer inserted into the thickest part of the thigh registers 165°F, 2½ to 3 hours. (Cover the bird loosely with foil if it browns too quickly, and add the broth to the pan if the vegetables begin to scorch.)

⑤ Carefully tilt the turkey to empty the juices from the cavity into the pan. Transfer the turkey to a carving board, cover loosely with foil and let rest for at least 25 minutes.

⑥ Reserve the pan and its contents for gravy. Carve the turkey as desired. Garnish with fresh herbs, if desired.

**PER SERVING** 441 CAL, 16 G FAT (4.5 G SAT FAT), 257 MG CHOL, 482 MG SOD, 69 G PRO, 0 G CAR, 0 G FIBER

# 1 *Bacon maple-orange turkey*

**ACTIVE** 30 MIN • **TOTAL** 4 HR • **SERVES** 8 (WITH LEFTOVERS) • COST PER SERVING $4.36

Prep and place the turkey and vegetables in the roasting pan as directed, but do not rub with oil. In a small bowl, whisk together ½ cup **pure maple syrup**, ¼ cup **fresh orange juice** and ½ tsp **salt**. Transfer one-third of the maple mixture to a second bowl and set aside. Brush half the remaining mixture all over the turkey. Lay 12 slices **thick-cut bacon** over the turkey breast on a diagonal, overlapping the slices slightly. Stick toothpicks into the ends of each bacon slice (this will keep them from curling as they cook). Brush 2 Tbsp maple mixture over the bacon. Cook the turkey as directed. Before resting, brush the bacon and turkey with the reserved maple mixture and remove the toothpicks.

PER SERVING 518 CAL, 19 G FAT (5.5 G SAT FAT), 267 MG CHOL, 493 MG SOD, 73 G PRO, 9 G CAR, 0 G FIBER

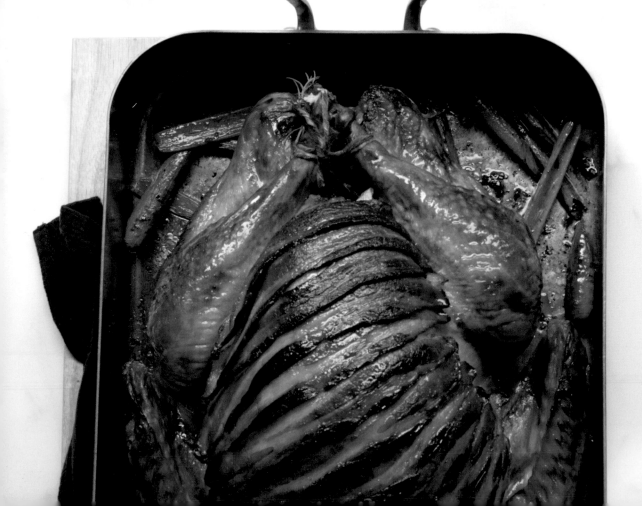

### 3 Red-rubbed turkey

**ACTIVE** 25 MIN • **TOTAL** 3 HR 50 MIN
**SERVES** 8 (WITH LEFTOVERS)
COST PER SERVING $4.07

Prep and place the turkey and
vegetables in the roasting pan as
directed, but do not rub with oil.
In a small bowl, combine 3 Tbsp
**smoked paprika**, 1 Tbsp each
**ground coriander** and **garlic
powder**, 2 tsp **salt** and 1 tsp
**cayenne pepper**. Mix in 2 Tbsp
**olive oil**. Rub all over the turkey
and cook as directed.

PER SERVING 451 CAL, 17 G FAT (4.5 G SAT FAT),
257 MG CHOL, 483 MG SOD, 70 G PRO, 2 G CAR,
1 G FIBER

### 2 Herb & lemon stuffed turkey

**ACTIVE** 30 MIN • **TOTAL** 4 HR • **SERVES** 8 (WITH LEFTOVERS)
COST PER SERVING $3.84

Prep the turkey and vegetables as directed,
but do not tie the legs. Using a vegetable
peeler, remove 6 strips of **zest** from 1 lemon.
Finely chop the zest (you should have about
2 Tbsp). Squeeze 2 Tbsp **lemon juice** into a
small bowl and whisk in 2 Tbsp **olive oil** and
1 Tbsp **Dijon mustard**. Stir in 4 cloves **garlic**
(finely chopped), 1 cup **fresh flat-leaf parsley**,
¼ cup **fresh sage leaves** (each chopped), 2
sprigs **fresh rosemary** (finely chopped) and
the zest. Carefully slide your fingers under the
skin of the turkey breast and thighs to loosen
it. Stuff the herb mixture under the skin. Place
the **lemon halves** in the cavity with the herbs
listed in the basic recipe, tie, rub with oil, sprinkle
with **salt** and cook as directed.

PER SERVING 466 CAL, 19 G FAT (5 G SAT FAT), 257 MG CHOL, 513 MG SOD,
69 G PRO, 1 G CAR, 0 G FIBER

p106

p101

p93

p93

p113

p102

p105

p108

p101

# Sides, Snacks & Drinks

# Super spuds

Give your potato salad a tasty update—or four!
These delicious sides will fit right in at your next
party, picnic or potluck.

START
HERE

## BASIC POTATO SALAD

**ACTIVE** 10 MIN • **TOTAL** 35 MIN • **SERVES** 6

2   lb small new potatoes
    (about 25)

    Kosher salt

    Vinaigrette or
    Creamy dressing
    (recipes, *below*)

½   cup fresh flat-leaf
    parsley, chopped

❶ Place the potatoes in a large, wide pot, cover with cold water
and bring to a boil. Add 2 tsp salt, reduce heat and simmer until
the potatoes are just tender, 10 to 15 minutes. Drain and run
under cold water to cool.

❷ While the potatoes are cooking, make the dressing.

❸ Cut the potatoes in half (or quarter if large). Add the potatoes
to the dressing and gently toss to coat. Fold in the parsley.

### BASIC VINAIGRETTE

In a large bowl, whisk together 3 Tbsp
**olive oil**, 2 Tbsp **red wine vinegar**,
1 Tbsp **Dijon mustard** and ¼ tsp each
**salt** and **pepper**.

### BASIC CREAMY DRESSING

In a large bowl, whisk together 3 Tbsp
**sour cream**, 2 Tbsp **mayonnaise**, 1 Tbsp
**white wine vinegar** and ¼ tsp each **salt**
and **pepper**.

# 1 *Chimichurri potato salad*

**ACTIVE** 20 MIN • **TOTAL** 35 MIN
**SERVES** 6
COST PER SERVING 59¢

Prepare the basic potato salad (shown with Vinaigrette). Fold in 1 small **red chile** and 1 small clove **garlic** (each finely chopped) along with 4 **scallions** and 4 strips **lemon zest** (each thinly sliced).

**PER SERVING** 194 CAL, 7 G FAT (1 G SAT FAT), 0 MG CHOL, 231 MG SOD, 4 G PRO, 29 G CAR, 2 G FIBER

## 2 *Potato salad with sweet corn, bacon & red onion*

**ACTIVE** 25 MIN • **TOTAL** 35 MIN
**SERVES** 6 • COST PER SERVING $1.08

Prepare the basic potato salad (shown with Vinaigrette). Toss with 1 cup **fresh corn kernals** (from 1 ear) and ½ small **red onion** (thinly sliced). Fold in 6 slices **bacon** (cooked and broken into pieces) and 2 cups **baby arugula** (roughly chopped).

**PER SERVING** 258 CAL, 10.5 G FAT (2 G SAT FAT), 9 MG CHOL, 375 MG SOD, 8 G PRO, 33 G CAR, 3 G FIBER

## 3 *Waldorf-style potato salad*

**ACTIVE** 20 MIN • **TOTAL** 35 MIN
**SERVES** 6 • COST PER SERVING 99¢

Prepare the basic potato salad (shown with Creamy dressing), whisking 1 Tbsp **whole-grain mustard** into the dressing. Toss the potato salad with 1 cup **small red grapes** (halved) and 4 stalks **celery** (thinly sliced). Fold in ½ cup **walnuts** (toasted and roughly chopped).

**PER SERVING** 260 CAL, 11 G FAT (2 G SAT FAT), 5 MG CHOL, 271 MG SOD, 6 G PRO, 35 G CAR, 4 G FIBER

## 4 *Tangy potato & egg salad*

**ACTIVE** 20 MIN • **TOTAL** 35 MIN
**SERVES** 6 • COST PER SERVING 53¢

Prepare the basic potato salad (shown with Creamy dressing), substituting fresh **dill** for the parsley. Fold in 4 large **hard-boiled eggs** (roughly chopped) and 2 **half-sour pickles** (cut into ¼-in. pieces).

**PER SERVING** 225 CAL, 8 G FAT (2 G SAT FAT), 129 MG CHOL, 419 MG SOD, 8 G PRO, 28 G CAR, 2 G FIBER

# The right stuffing

Make a classic herb variation or dress it up with everything from bacon and chestnuts to apples and pecans.

## BASIC HERB STUFFING

**ACTIVE** 20 MIN • **TOTAL** 45 MIN • **SERVES** 8 TO 10 • **COST PER SERVING** $1.18

3   Tbsp olive oil, plus more for the pan

1   small loaf country bread (about 1 lb), cut into ½-in. pieces (about 10 cups)

2   medium onions, chopped
    Kosher salt and pepper

2   large carrots, cut into ¼-in. pieces

2   stalks celery, cut into ¼-in. pieces

3   cups low-sodium chicken broth

1   cup fresh flat-leaf parsley, chopped

2   tsp fresh thyme leaves

2   large eggs, beaten

❶ Heat oven to 375°F. Oil a 3-qt casserole dish. Place the bread on a rimmed baking sheet and toast until golden brown, 15 to 20 minutes; transfer to a large bowl.

❷ Meanwhile, heat the oil in a large skillet over medium heat. Add the onions, 1 tsp salt and ½ tsp pepper and cook, covered, stirring occasionally, until very tender and beginning to turn golden, 6 to 8 minutes.

❸ Add the carrots and celery and cook, stirring occasionally, until tender, 6 to 7 minutes. Add the broth and bring to a boil. Stir in the parsley and thyme.

❹ Transfer the vegetable mixture to the bowl and toss with the bread. Fold in the beaten eggs. Transfer to the prepared baking dish, cover with foil and bake for 10 minutes. Remove the foil and bake until golden brown, 15 to 20 minutes more.

**PER SERVING** 229 CAL, 8 G FAT (1 G SAT FAT), 41 MG CHOL, 600 MG SOD, 8 G PRO, 31 G CAR, 3 G FIBER

# ❶ Apple, pecan & dill stuffing

**ACTIVE** 25 MIN • **TOTAL** 50 MIN
**SERVES** 8 TO 10
**COST PER SERVING** $1.58

Prepare the stuffing with the following changes: Omit the thyme. Core and cut 1 large **Jonagold**, **Idared** or **Gala apple** into ½-in. pieces. Add it to the bread mixture along with 1 cup **pecans** (roughly chopped) and ¼ cup **fresh dill** (roughly chopped) and toss to combine. Bake as directed.

**PER SERVING** 317 CAL, 16 G FAT (2 G SAT FAT), 41 MG CHOL, 600 MG SOD, 9 G PRO, 36 G CAR, 4 G FIBER

# ❷ Sausage, dried cherry & sage stuffing

**ACTIVE** 25 MIN • **TOTAL** 50 MIN
**SERVES** 8 TO 10
**COST PER SERVING** $2.15

Prepare the stuffing with the following changes: Omit the thyme. Cook ¾ lb **Italian sausage** (casings removed) in a skillet over medium heat, breaking it up with a spoon, until no longer pink, about 5 minutes. Stir in ¼ cup **fresh sage** (chopped) and ¾ cup **dried cherries**. Add the sausage mixture to the bread mixture and toss to combine. Bake as directed.

**PER SERVING** 258 CAL, 20 G FAT (6 G SAT FAT), 70 MG CHOL, 876 MG SOD, 13 G PRO, 40 G CAR, 5 G FIBER

# ❸ Bacon & chestnut stuffing

**ACTIVE** 30 MIN • **TOTAL** 55 MIN
**SERVES** 8 TO 10
**COST PER SERVING** $2.37

Prepare the stuffing with the following changes: Cut ¾ lb sliced **bacon** into 1-in. pieces and cook in a large skillet over medium heat until crisp, about 8 minutes. Transfer to a paper towel–lined plate. Add the bacon and 1 cup **jarred chestnuts** (crumbled) to the bread mixture and toss to combine. Bake as directed.

**PER SERVING** 336 CAL, 14 G FAT (3 G SAT FAT), 55 MG CHOL, 888 MG SOD, 13 G PRO, 40 G CAR, 3 G FIBER

# Great-for-you grains

Choose a healthy whole grain like barley, brown rice, quinoa or bulgur, then use it as the base for one of these amazing sides.

## HOW TO COOK GRAINS

**Barley:** 1 cup dry = 3 cups cooked
Cook 1 cup pearl barley in a medium pot of boiling water until tender, 20 to 25 minutes (semi- or unpearled barley can take 30 to 40 minutes). Drain.

**Bulgur:** 1 cup dry = 3½ cups cooked
In a small saucepan, combine 1 cup bulgur with 2 cups water. Bring to a boil, add ½ tsp salt, reduce heat and simmer, covered, until tender, 12 to 15 minutes. Drain any excess liquid and fluff with a fork.

**Quinoa:** 1 cup dry = 3½ cups cooked
Rinse the quinoa well (it has a bitter outer layer). In a medium saucepan, combine 1 cup quinoa with 2 cups water. Bring to a boil, add ½ tsp salt, reduce heat and simmer, covered until all the liquid is absorbed, 15 to 20 minutes. Fluff with a fork.

**Wheat berries:** 1 cup dry = 2½ cups cooked
Cook 1 cup wheat berries in a large pot of boiling water until tender, 60 to 75 minutes. Drain and rinse.

## ❶ Sautéed leeks, peas & parsley

**ACTIVE** 25 MIN • **TOTAL** 30 MIN
**SERVES** 4 TO 6
**COST PER SERVING** 66¢

Heat 2 Tbsp **olive oil** in a medium skillet over medium heat. Add 2 **leeks** (white and light green parts only, cut into ½-in.-thick half-moons). Season with ¼ tsp each **salt** and **pepper** and cook, stirring occasionally, until tender, 7 to 8 minutes. Add 1 cup **frozen peas** (thawed) and 2 tsp grated **lemon zest** and cook, stirring occasionally, until heated through, about 3 minutes; stir in ½ cup **fresh flat-leaf parsley** (chopped). Fold the mixture into 2½ to 3 cups **cooked grains** (pearl barley shown).

♥ **PER SERVING** 195 CAL, 5 G FAT (1 G SAT FAT), 0 MG CHOL, 92 MG SOD, 5 G, PRO, 34 G CAR, 7 G FIBER

## ② Roasted red pepper, green beans & red onion

**ACTIVE** 10 MIN • **TOTAL** 25 MIN
**SERVES** 4 TO 6
**COST PER SERVING** 83¢

In a large bowl, toss 2 jarred **roasted red peppers** (rinsed and cut into ¼-in. pieces), 4 oz **green beans** (cut into 1-in. pieces) and ½ **red onion** (finely chopped) with 1 Tbsp **olive oil**, 2 tsp **red wine vinegar** and ¼ tsp each **salt** and **pepper**. Fold mixture into 2½ to 3 cups **cooked grains** (quinoa shown).

**PER SERVING** 139 CAL, 4 G FAT (1 G SAT FAT), 0 MG CHOL, 336 MG SOD, 5 G, PRO, 22 G CAR, 3 G FIBER

## ③ Creamy spiced carrot & raisin

**ACTIVE** 15 MIN • **TOTAL** 25 MIN
**SERVES** 4 TO 6
**COST PER SERVING** 44¢

In a large bowl, whisk together ⅓ cup **nonfat Greek yogurt**, 1 tsp **orange zest**, 3 Tbsp fresh **orange juice**, ½ tsp each **ground cumin** and **salt** and ¼ tsp **pepper**. Add 2½ to 3 cups **cooked grains** (bulgur shown) and gently toss to coat. Fold in 2 medium **carrots** (coarsely grated), ½ cup **golden raisins** and ½ cup **fresh cilantro** (roughly chopped).

**PER SERVING** 141 CAL, 0 G FAT (0 G SAT FAT), 0 MG CHOL, 315 MG SOD, 5 G, PRO, 32 G CAR, 6 G FIBER

## ④ Thyme-roasted grapes & spinach

**ACTIVE** 15 MIN • **TOTAL** 1 HR
**SERVES** 4 TO 6
**COST PER SERVING** 94¢

Heat oven to 400°F. On a rimmed baking sheet, toss 1 lb small **seedless red grapes**, 6 small sprigs **fresh thyme**, 1 Tbsp **olive oil** and ¼ tsp each **salt** and **pepper**. Roast, tossing occasionally, until the grapes begin to burst, 15 minutes. Scatter 1 bunch **spinach** (thick stems discarded) over the grapes and roast for 2 minutes more. Gently toss until spinach is beginning to wilt. Fold the mixture into 2½ to 3 cups **cooked grains** (wheat berries shown).

♥ **PER SERVING** 194 CAL, 3 G FAT (0 G SAT FAT), 0 MG CHOL, 116 MG SOD, 6 G, PRO, 37 G CAR, 5 G FIBER

# Between the fold

Wrap store-bought dough around favorite fillings for loads of flavor with hardly any effort.

**START HERE**

## BASIC EMPANADAS

**ACTIVE** 10 MIN • **TOTAL** 35 MIN • **MAKES** 10

All-purpose flour, for rolling

2 refrigerated rolled pie crusts

Filling (see recipes, this and following page)

1 large egg

Salsa or hot sauce, for serving

❶ Heat oven to 400°F. Line a baking sheet with parchment.

❷ On a lightly floured surface, roll the pie crust into a 14-in. circle. Using a 5-in. round cutter, cut out 5 circles, rerolling the scraps as necessary. Repeat with the remaining pie crust.

❸ Divide the filling among the circles (about 2 Tbsp each), placing it toward one side. Lightly brush the edges of the rounds with water. Fold the dough over the filling and crimp or lightly press with a fork to seal. Transfer to the prepared baking sheet.

❹ In a small bowl, beat the egg with 1 Tbsp water. Brush the empanadas with the egg mixture and bake until golden brown, 20 to 23 minutes. Let cool for 5 minutes. Serve with salsa or hot sauce, if desired.

## ❶ *Spiced beef empanadas*

**ACTIVE** 15 MIN • **TOTAL** 20 MIN
**MAKES** 10
**COST PER EMPANADA** 50¢

In a large skillet, sauté 1 small **onion** (finely chopped) in 1 Tbsp **olive oil** until tender and beginning to brown, 6 to 8 minutes. Add 1 clove **garlic** (finely chopped) and sauté for 1 minute. Add 6 oz **lean ground beef** and cook, breaking it up with a spoon, until cooked through, 4 to 5 minutes. Stir in 1 tsp each **ground coriander** and **cumin**, ⅛ tsp **cayenne pepper** and ¼ tsp **salt**; cook for 1 minute. Add ¼ cup **tomato sauce** and bring to a boil. Reduce the heat and simmer for 2 minutes. Remove from the heat and stir in ¼ cup **frozen peas** (thawed). Assemble the empanadas as directed. Sprinkle with ¼ cup grated **sharp Cheddar** and bake as directed.

**PER EMPANADA** 190 CAL, 13.5 G FAT (6 G SAT FAT), 36 MG CHOL, 273 MG SOD, 6 G PRO, 15 G CAR, 0 G FIBER

## ② *Zesty sausage & pepper empanadas*

**ACTIVE** 20 MIN • **TOTAL** 20 MIN • **MAKES** 10
**COST PER EMPANADA** 42¢

Heat 1 Tbsp **olive oil** in a large skillet over medium heat. Add 1 small **onion** (finely chopped) and cook, covered, until tender, 4 to 6 minutes. Add 4 oz **sweet Italian sausage** (1 to 2 links, casings removed) and cook, breaking it up with a spoon, until browned and cooked through, 6 to 8 minutes. During the last 2 minutes of cooking, add 1 clove **garlic** (finely chopped). Stir in ½ tsp **paprika**, ¼ tsp each **ground cumin**, **dried oregano** and **chili powder**, and ¼ tsp each **salt** and **pepper** and cook, stirring, for 1 minute. Remove from the heat and add 1 **roasted red pepper** (chopped) and toss to combine. Assemble and bake the empanadas as directed.

**PER EMPANADA** 166 CAL, 11 G FAT (5.5 G SAT FAT), 25 MG CHOL, 289 MG SOD, 3 G PRO, 15 G CAR, 0 G FIBER

## ③ *Black bean, cheese & corn empanadas*

**ACTIVE** 10 MIN • **TOTAL** 15 MIN • **MAKES** 10
**COST PER EMPANADA** 53¢

In a large skillet, sauté 1 small **onion** (finely chopped) and 1 small **poblano pepper** (cut into ¼-in. pieces) in 1 Tbsp **olive oil** until tender and the onion is beginning to brown, 6 to 8 minutes. Add 1 clove **garlic** (finely chopped) and cook, stirring, for 1 minute. Remove from the heat and stir in ¾ cup canned **black beans** (rinsed), ¼ cup frozen **corn** kernels (thawed) and 1 Tbsp **fresh lime juice**; let cool for 5 minutes. Stir in 2 oz **Monterey Jack cheese** (grated) and 1 Tbsp **sour cream**, then ¼ cup **fresh cilantro** (roughly chopped). Assemble and bake the empanadas as directed.

**PER EMPANADA** 185 CAL, 11.5 G FAT (6 G SAT FAT), 28 MG CHOL, 267 MG SOD, 4 G PRO, 19 G CAR, 1 G FIBER

## ④ *Chicken, raisin & green olive empanadas*

**ACTIVE** 10 MIN • **TOTAL** 20 MIN • **MAKES** 10
COST PER EMPANADA 57¢

In a small bowl, combine ⅓ cup **boiling water** with ½ tsp **ground turmeric**, ½ tsp **paprika** and ½ tsp **ancho chili powder**. Add ¼ cup **raisins** and let cool to room temperature. In a medium bowl, combine 1 cup finely shredded **rotisserie chicken**, 1 **scallion** (thinly sliced), 4 **pitted green olives** (sliced), ¼ cup **fresh cilantro** (chopped), 1 Tbsp **fresh lime juice** and ¼ tsp **salt**. Add the raisin mixture and toss to combine. Assemble and bake the empanadas as directed.

PER EMPANADA 172 CAL, 9.5 G FAT (5 G SAT FAT), 34 MG CHOL, 285 MG SOD, 6 G PRO, 16 G CAR, 0 G FIBER

## ⑤ *Dulce de leche & banana empanadas*

**ACTIVE** 10 MIN • **TOTAL** 20 MIN • **MAKES** 10
COST PER EMPANADA 44¢

Spread each pastry circle with 1 Tbsp **dulce de leche**, leaving a ½ in. border. Top each with ¼ **banana** (thinly sliced). Seal and bake as directed. Drizzle with **melted chocolate** before serving, if desired.

PER EMPANADA 221 CAL, 10 G FAT (5.5 G SAT FAT), 28 MG CHOL, 187 MG SOD, 3 G PRO, 32 G CAR, 1 G FIBER

# Dip in

## Five festive twists that take salsa beyond corn chips.

**START HERE**

## CHUNKY SALSA

**ACTIVE** 15 MIN • **TOTAL** 15 MIN • **SERVES** 6 • **COST PER SERVING** 33¢

- 2  jalapeños (seeded for less heat, if desired), finely chopped
- 1  small clove garlic, finely chopped
- ½  medium white onion, finely chopped
   Kosher salt and pepper
- 1  lb plum tomatoes (about 5), seeded and cut into ¼-in. pieces
- 2  Tbsp fresh lime juice
- 1  Tbsp olive oil
- ½  cup fresh cilantro, chopped

In a large bowl, combine the jalapeños, garlic, onion, ½ tsp salt and ¼ tsp pepper. Add the tomatoes, lime juice and oil and toss to combine. Fold in the cilantro.

**PER SERVING** 41 CAL, 2.5 G FAT (0.5 G SAT FAT), 0 MG CHOL, 166 MG SOD, 1 G PRO, 5 G CAR, 1.5 G FIBER

## ❶ *Charred corn salsa*

**ACTIVE** 15 MIN • **TOTAL** 20 MIN
**SERVES** 6
**COST PER SERVING** 36¢

Prepare the chunky salsa with the following changes: Omit the white onion and tomatoes. Heat grill to medium-high. Brush 2 ears **corn** and 1 medium **red onion** (cut into 1-in. wedges) with **olive oil** and season with ¼ tsp each **salt** and **pepper**. Grill, turning occasionally, until slightly charred and tender, 3 to 4 minutes for the corn and 8 to 10 minutes for the onion. Transfer to a cutting board. Cut the corn off the cob and chop the red onion. Fold into the vegetable mixture.

**PER SERVING** 60 CAL, 3 G FAT (0.5 G SAT FAT), 0 MG CHOL, 248 MG SOD, 2 G PRO, 9 G CAR, 1 G FIBER

## ② *Crunchy garden salsa*

**ACTIVE** 20 MIN • **TOTAL** 20 MIN • **SERVES** 6
COST PER SERVING 54¢

Prepare the chunky salsa with the following changes:
Reduce the tomatoes to ½ lb, omit the cilantro and
fold in 2 **Kirby cucumbers** (cut into ¼-in. pieces),
6 **radishes** (thinly sliced into half-moons) and ½ cup
**fresh mint** (chopped).

♥ **PER SERVING** 41 CAL, 2.5 G FAT (0.5 G SAT FAT), 0 MG CHOL, 168 MG SOD,
1 G PRO, 4.5 G CAR, 1.5 G FIBER

## ③ *Roasted tomato salsa*

**ACTIVE** 15 MIN • **TOTAL** 25 MIN • **SERVES** 6
COST PER SERVING 38¢

Assemble the ingredients for the chunky salsa, but
do not chop. Heat oven to 425°F. Cut the **tomatoes**
and **jalapeños** in half (seed for less heat, if desired).
Cut the **onion** into 1-in. pieces. On a large rimmed
baking sheet, toss the tomatoes, jalapeños, onion
and **garlic** with 2 Tbsp **olive oil**, ¾ tsp **salt** and ¼
tsp **pepper**. Roast until the vegetables are tender and
beginning to brown, 10 to 15 minutes. Transfer the
vegetables to a food processor, add the **cilantro** and
purée until finely chopped. Add the **lime juice** and
pulse to combine.

**PER SERVING** 61 CAL, 5 G FAT (4 G SAT FAT), 0 MG CHOL, 246 MG SOD,
1 G PRO, 5 G CAR, 1.5 G FIBER

## ④ *Black bean & avocado salsa*

**ACTIVE** 15 MIN • **TOTAL** 15 MIN • **SERVES** 6
COST PER SERVING 53¢

Prepare the chunky salsa with the following changes:
Omit the tomatoes. Toss the vegetable mixture with
a 15.5-oz can **black beans** (rinsed) and 2 **scallions**
(thinly sliced). Fold in 1 **avocado** (diced) along with
the **cilantro**.

**PER SERVING** 133 CAL, 6 G FAT (1 G SAT FAT), 0 MG CHOL, 333 MG SOD,
5 G PRO, 16 G CAR, 7 G FIBER

## ⑤ *Peach, red onion & basil salsa*

**ACTIVE** 15 MIN • **TOTAL** 15 MIN • **SERVES** 6
COST PER SERVING 42¢

Prepare the chunky salsa with the following changes:
Omit the garlic and cilantro. Reduce the tomatoes to
½ lb and substitute 1 small **red onion** for the white
onion. Fold in ½ lb **peaches** or **nectarines** (cut into
¼-in. pieces) and ½ cup **fresh basil** (roughly chopped).

♥ **PER SERVING** 48 CAL, 2.5 G FAT (0.5 G SAT FAT), 0 MG CHOL, 164 MG SOD,
1 G PRO, 7 G CAR, 1 G FIBER

# Nice tea

Spiff up this classic thirst quencher with
fruit and other delicious add-ins.

**START HERE**

### BASIC ICED TEA CONCENTRATE

**ACTIVE** 5 MIN • **TOTAL** 1 HR
**MAKES** 4 CUPS • (ENOUGH
FOR 6 TO 8 SERVINGS)
**COST PER SERVING** 5¢

8   **black, red or green
tea bags**

Bring 4 cups water
to a boil in a medium
saucepan. Remove from
heat, add the tea bags
and let steep, stirring
twice, for 4 minutes.
Discard the tea bags and
let the tea cool.

### ①Pineapple & thyme iced tea

**ACTIVE** 5 MIN • **TOTAL** 1 HR • **SERVES** 8
**COST PER SERVING** 27¢

Make the basic tea concentrate with the following changes: Add the tea bags to the water along with 2 large sprigs **fresh thyme**; steep and cool as directed. Discard the thyme and stir in ½ **pineapple** (cored and cut into ½-in. pieces) and 4 cups **cold water**. Serve over ice with additional thyme, if desired. (Shown with green tea.)

### ②Double apple iced tea

**ACTIVE** 5 MIN • **TOTAL** 1 HR • **SERVES** 8
**COST PER SERVING** 25¢

Make the basic tea concentrate. Core and slice 2 crisp **apples** (such as Granny Smith or Braeburn). Stir them into the tea concentrate along with 4 cups **apple juice**. Serve over ice. (Shown with black tea.)

### ③Strawberry iced tea slushie

**ACTIVE** 10 MIN • **TOTAL** 1 HR • **SERVES** 6
**COST PER SERVING** 57¢

Make the basic tea concentrate. In a blender, purée 8 oz frozen **strawberries**, 2 cups tea concentrate and 1 cup **ice** until smooth. Transfer to 3 glasses. Repeat. (Shown with Red Zinger tea.)

### **4** *Honeydew & watermelon iced tea*

**ACTIVE** 5 MIN • **TOTAL** 1 HR • **SERVES** 8
**COST PER SERVING** 17¢

Make the basic tea concentrate. Stir in 1 cup each **watermelon** (cut into 1-in. pieces) and **honeydew** (thinly sliced) and 4 cups **cold water**. Serve over ice. (Shown with green tea.)

### **5** *Honey, ginger & nectarine iced tea*

**ACTIVE** 5 MIN • **TOTAL** 1 HR • **SERVES** 8
**COST PER SERVING** 21¢

Make the basic tea concentrate with the following changes: Add the tea bags to the water along with a 1-in. piece **fresh ginger** (thinly sliced), 2 Tbsp **honey** and ½ **lemon** (thinly sliced); steep and cool as directed. Discard the ginger and lemon. Stir in 2 **nectarines** (each cut into 8 wedges), ½ **lemon** (thinly sliced) and 4 cups **cold water**. Serve over ice. (Shown with Red Zinger tea.)

### **6** *Cucumber, lemon & mint fizz*

**ACTIVE** 5 MIN • **TOTAL** 1 HR • **SERVES** 8
**COST PER SERVING** 25¢

Make the basic tea concentrate with the following changes: Add the tea bags to the water along with 4 sprigs **fresh mint** and ½ **lemon** (thinly sliced); steep and cool as directed. Discard the mint and lemon. Stir in ½ **seedless cucumber** (thinly sliced), ½ **lemon** (thinly sliced) and 4 cups **ginger ale**. Serve over ice with additional mint, if desired. (Shown with black tea.)

p127

p131

p133

p123

p135

p117

p119

p131

p126

# Sweets & Baked Goods

# Butter up

Flavor-packed and bursting with delicious ingredients, these scones are meant to be savored.

**START HERE**

## BASIC SCONES

**ACTIVE** 15 MIN • **TOTAL** 30 MIN • **MAKES** 8 SCONES • **COST PER SCONE** 20¢

| | |
|---|---|
| 2 | cups all-purpose flour |
| 2 | Tbsp granulated sugar |
| 1 | Tbsp baking powder |
| ½ | tsp kosher salt |
| 6 | Tbsp cold unsalted butter, cut into small pieces |
| 1 | large egg |
| ½ | cup plus 1 Tbsp heavy cream |

❶ Heat oven to 425°F. Line a baking sheet with parchment.

❷ In a large bowl, whisk together the flour, sugar, baking powder and salt. Add the butter and, using a pastry blender or two knives, cut it in until the mixture forms small crumbs. Make a well in the center of the mixture.

❸ In a bowl, whisk together the egg and ½ cup heavy cream. Add to the flour mixture and, using a fork, gently stir until incorporated (do not overmix). Bring the dough together.

❹ On a lightly floured surface, shape the dough into an 8-in. round (about 1 in. thick), cut into wedges and place on the prepared baking sheet. Brush the tops with the remaining 1 Tbsp cream and bake until golden brown, 12 to 14 minutes.

**PER SCONE** 274 CAL, 16 G FAT (10 G SAT FAT), 69 MG CHOL, 344 MG SOD, 4 G PRO, 29 G CAR, 1 G FIBER

## 1 *Cranberry-oat scones*

**ACTIVE** 15 MIN • **TOTAL** 30 MIN • **MAKES** 8 SCONES
**COST PER SCONE** 47¢

Prepare the basic scones with the following changes: Cut in the butter, then fold in 1 cup **old-fashioned oats**, ½ cup **dried cranberries** and ¼ cup **crystallized ginger** (finely chopped). On a lightly floured surface, shape the dough into an 8 x 4-in. rectangle (about 1 in. thick). Cut into eight 2-in. rectangles and place on the prepared baking sheet. Brush the tops with 1 Tbsp **heavy cream** and sprinkle with additional oats, if desired. Bake until golden brown, 12 to 14 minutes.

**PER SCONE** 352 CAL, 17 G FAT (10 G SAT FAT), 69 MG CHOL, 346 MG SOD, 6 G PRO, 46 G CAR, 2 G FIBER

## ② *Cheddar-jalapeño scones*

**ACTIVE** 20 MIN • **TOTAL** 35 MIN • **MAKES** 8 SCONES
COST PER SCONE 36¢

Prepare the basic scones with the following changes:
Cut in the butter, then fold in 4 oz **sharp orange
Cheddar** (coarsely grated; 1 cup), 2 **jalapeños**
(seeded and finely chopped) and 2 **scallions** (finely
chopped). On a lightly floured surface, shape the
dough into an 8-in. round (about 1 in. thick). Using a
2½-in. round cookie cutter, cut the dough into circles
and place on the prepared baking sheet. Reshape
and cut the scraps. Brush the tops with 1 Tbsp **heavy
cream** and bake until golden brown, 10 to 12 minutes.

PER SCONE 331 CAL, 20 G FAT (13 G SAT FAT), 82 MG CHOL, 436 MG SOD,
8 G PRO, 29 G CAR, 1 G FIBER

## ③ *Sour cream-chocolate chip scones*

**ACTIVE** 15 MIN • **TOTAL** 30 MIN • **MAKES** 8 SCONES
COST PER SCONE 51¢

Prepare the basic scones with the following changes:
Increase **sugar** to ¼ cup. Cut in the butter, then fold in
1¼ cups **semisweet chocolate chips**. Replace the ½
cup heavy cream with ¾ cup **sour cream** and whisk 1
tsp **pure vanilla extract** into the sour cream and egg
mixture. On a lightly floured surface, shape the dough
into an 8-in. round (about 1 in. thick). Cut into 8 wedges
and place on the prepared baking sheet. Brush the tops
with 1 Tbsp **heavy cream** and bake until golden brown,
12 to 14 minutes.

PER SCONE 390 CAL, 21 G FAT (12 G SAT FAT), 56 MG CHOL, 355 MG SOD,
6 G PRO, 49 G CAR, 2 G FIBER

## ④ *Maple-pecan scones*

ACTIVE 15 MIN • TOTAL 30 MIN • MAKES 8 SCONES
COST PER SCONE 83¢

Prepare the basic scones with the following changes:
Replace the granulated sugar with ¼ cup packed **dark brown sugar**. Whisk 1 tsp **ground cinnamon** into the flour mixture. Cut in the butter, then fold in 1 cup **pecans** (roughly chopped). Reduce heavy cream to ¼ cup and whisk ¼ cup **pure maple syrup** into the egg and cream mixture. On a lightly floured surface, shape the dough into an 8 x 4-in. rectangle (about 1 in. thick). Cut into eight 2-in. rectangles and place on the prepared baking sheet. In a small bowl, whisk together 1 Tbsp each **pure maple syrup** and **heavy cream**. Brush the mixture over the tops and bake until golden brown, 12 to 14 minutes.

PER SCONE 389 CAL, 23 G FAT (9 G SAT FAT), 59 MG CHOL, 344 MG SOD, 6 G PRO, 42 G CAR, 2 G FIBER

## ⑤ *Orange-rosemary scones*

ACTIVE 20 MIN • TOTAL 35 MIN • MAKES 16 SCONES
COST PER SCONE 14¢

Prepare the basic scones with the following changes:
Using a vegetable peeler, remove 3 strips of **zest** from 1 **navel orange**. Thinly slice the zest. Cut in the butter, then fold in the zest and 1 Tbsp **fresh rosemary** (roughly chopped). On a lightly floured surface, shape the dough into two 5-in. rounds. Cut each into 8 wedges (16 total) and place on the prepared baking sheet. Brush the tops with 1 Tbsp **heavy cream** and bake until golden brown, 8 to 12 minutes.

PER SCONE 138 CAL, 8 G FAT (5 G SAT FAT), 35 MG CHOL, 172 MG SOD, 2 G PRO, 14 G CAR, 1 G FIBER

# Healthy muffins

These breakfast treats pack loads of fiber and goodness into delicious little packages.

**START
HERE**

## BASIC HEALTHY MUFFINS

**ACTIVE** 10 MIN • **TOTAL** 35 MIN • **MAKES** 10 MUFFINS • **COST PER MUFFIN** 14¢

| | |
|---|---|
| 1 | cup wheat bran |
| 1 | cup whole-wheat flour |
| ½ | cup granulated sugar |
| 1 | tsp baking powder |
| ½ | tsp baking soda |
| ½ | tsp ground cinnamon |
| | Pinch kosher salt |
| ½ | cup unsweetened applesauce |
| ½ | cup lowfat buttermilk |
| ¼ | cup olive oil |
| 1 | large egg |

**1** Heat oven to 350°F and line a 12-hole muffin pan with 10 paper liners (leave 2 holes empty).

**2** In a medium bowl, combine the dry ingredients: wheat bran, flour, sugar, baking powder, baking soda, cinnamon and salt.

**3** In a large bowl, combine the wet ingredients: applesauce, buttermilk, oil and egg.

**4** Add the dry ingredients to the wet ingredients and mix just until combined.

**5** Divide the batter among the lined muffin cups and bake until a wooden pick inserted in the center comes out clean, 20 to 22 minutes. Let cool in the pan for 5 minutes, then transfer to a wire rack to cool completely.

**♥ PER MUFFIN** 158 CAL, 6.5 G FAT (1 G SAT FAT), 19 MG CHOL, 132 MG SOD, 4 G PRO, 25 G CAR, 4 G FIBER

# ① Carrot, cranberry & pecan muffins

**ACTIVE** 20 MIN • **TOTAL** 50 MIN • **MAKES** 10 MUFFINS • **COST PER MUFFIN** 32¢

Prepare the basic muffins with the following changes: Decrease the **applesauce** to ¼ cup. After combining the dry and wet ingredients, fold in 1 cup **fresh** or **frozen cranberries** (thawed, if frozen), 1 medium **carrot** and 1 medium **parsnip** (both peeled and grated; ½ cup each) and 2 tsp finely grated **fresh ginger**. Divide the batter among the lined muffin cups, top with ¼ cup **pecans** (roughly chopped) and bake until a wooden pick inserted in the center comes out clean, 25 to 27 minutes. Cool as directed.

❤ **PER MUFFIN** 190 CAL, 8.5 G FAT (1 G SAT FAT), 19 MG CHOL, 137 MG SOD, 4 G PRO, 27 G CAR, 5 G FIBER

## ② *Mini mocha chip muffins*

**ACTIVE** 20 MIN • **TOTAL** 40 MIN
**MAKES** 10 MUFFINS OR 24 MINI MUFFINS
COST PER MUFFIN 10¢

Prepare the basic muffins with the following changes: Add 2 tsp **instant espresso powder** to the wet ingredients. After combining the dry and wet ingredients, fold in ¼ cup **mini chocolate chips**. Divide the batter between two 12-hole mini muffin tin and bake until a wooden pick inserted in the center comes out clean, 14 to 16 minutes.

♥ **PER MINI MUFFIN** 78 CAL, 3.5 G FAT (1 G SAT FAT), 8 MG CHOL, 55 MG SOD, 2 G PRO, 12 G CAR, 2 G FIBER

## ③ *Pear & orange muffins*

**ACTIVE** 20 MIN • **TOTAL** 55 MIN
**MAKES** 10 MUFFINS
COST PER MUFFIN 26¢

In a small bowl, combine 2 tsp **granulated sugar** with 2 tsp **orange zest**. Prepare the basic muffins with the following changes: Decrease the **applesauce** to ¼ cup. After combining the dry and wet ingredients, fold in ½ medium ripe **red pear** (cut into ¼-in. pieces). Divide the batter among the lined muffin cups. Top with ½ medium **red pear** (halved crosswise; thinly sliced), then sprinkle with the orange sugar. Bake until a wooden pick inserted in the center comes out clean, 25 to 30 minutes. Cool as directed.

♥ **PER MUFFIN** 169 CAL, 6.5 G FAT (1 G SAT FAT), 19 MG CHOL, 132 MG SOD, 4 G PRO, 28 G CAR, 4 G FIBER

## ④ *Peanut butter & jelly muffins*

**ACTIVE** 20 MIN • **TOTAL** 50 MIN
**MAKES** 10 MUFFINS
COST PER MUFFIN 28¢

Prepare the basic muffins with the following changes: Decrease the **applesauce** to ¼ cup. After combining the dry and wet ingredients, fold in 1 cup **small red seedless grapes** (halved). Divide half the batter among the lined muffin cups. Top each with 1 tsp **creamy peanut butter**, then the remaining batter. Bake until a wooden pick inserted in the center comes out clean, 25 to 27 minutes. Cool as directed. In a small saucepan, combine ¼ cup **seedless jam** or **jelly** with 1 Tbsp **water**. Cook, stirring, over medium heat until melted and smooth. Just before serving, drizzle the jam mixture on the muffins.

♥ **PER MUFFIN** 220 CAL, 9 G FAT (2 G SAT FAT), 19 MG CHOL, 159 MG SOD, 5 G PRO, 33 G CAR, 4 G FIBER

# Quick and tasty breads

On the breakfast table or as an after-dinner treat, these sweet loaves take just 15 minutes to prep.

START
HERE

## BASIC WALNUT QUICK BREAD

**ACTIVE** 15 MIN • **TOTAL** 1 HR 15 MIN PLUS COOLING • **SERVES** 10 • **COST PER SERVING** 48¢

| | |
|---|---|
| | Cooking spray |
| 1¾ | cups all-purpose flour |
| 1¼ | tsp baking powder |
| ½ | tsp ground cinnamon |
| ½ | tsp kosher salt |
| 2 | large eggs |
| 1 | cup sour cream |
| ¾ | cup granulated sugar |
| ½ | cup canola oil |
| 1 | tsp pure vanilla extract |
| 1 | cup walnuts, chopped |

❶ Heat oven to 350°F. Coat an 8½ x 4½-in. loaf pan with cooking spray.

❷ In a medium bowl, whisk together the flour, baking powder, cinnamon and salt. In a large bowl, whisk together the eggs, sour cream, sugar, oil and vanilla.

❸ Gradually add the flour mixture into the egg mixture, stirring until just incorporated. Fold in the nuts.

❹ Transfer the batter to the prepared pan and bake until golden brown and a wooden pick inserted into the center comes out clean, 55 to 65 minutes. Let cool in the pan for 5 minutes before transferring to a wire rack to cool completely.

**PER SERVING** 367 CAL, 24 G FAT (4 G SAT FAT), 47 MG CHOL, 172 MG SOD, 6 G PRO, 34 G CAR, 1 G FIBER

# ❶ *Mini banana-coconut breads*

**ACTIVE** 15 MIN • **TOTAL** 1 HR 15 MIN PLUS COOLING • **SERVES** 10
COST PER SERVING 57¢

Prepare the basic quick bread with the following changes: Increase the **flour** to 2 cups and reduce the **sour cream** to ¾ cup. Add ¾ cup mashed ripe **banana** (about 2) to the egg mixture and fold in ½ cup **shredded coconut** along with the walnuts. Transfer the batter to three 5¾- by 3¼-in loaf pans (coated with cooking spray) and sprinkle the top of each with 2 Tbsp **shredded coconut**. Bake and cool as directed.

**PER SERVING** 413 CAL, 25 G FAT (5 G SAT FAT), 45 MG CHOL, 184 SOD, 6 G PRO, 43 G CAR, 2 G FIBER

# ❷ *Lemon-poppy seed bread*

**ACTIVE** 15 MIN • **TOTAL** 1 HR 15 MIN PLUS COOLING • **SERVES** 10
COST PER SERVING 36¢

Prepare the basic quick bread with the following changes: Omit the cinnamon and walnuts. Substitute 1 cup **lemon yogurt** (we used Dannon) for the sour cream. Add 2 tsp grated **lemon zest** and 1 Tbsp **poppy seeds** to the egg mixture. Bake as directed. While the bread bakes, in a small bowl, combine ¾ cup **confectioners' sugar** and 2 Tbsp **fresh lemon juice**. While the bread is still warm on the wire rack, spoon the glaze over the top.

**PER SERVING** 315 CAL, 13 G FAT (1 G SAT FAT), 38 MG CHOL, 173 MG SOD, 5 G PRO, 45 G CAR, 1 G FIBER

## ❸ *Carrot-raisin bread*

**ACTIVE** 15 MIN • **TOTAL** 1 HR 15 MIN PLUS COOLING • **SERVES** 10
**COST PER SERVING** 41¢

Prepare the basic quick bread with the following changes: Omit the walnuts. Increase the **flour** to 2 cups and the **cinnamon** to 1 tsp. Reduce the **sour cream** to ¾ cup and substitute ¾ cup packed **dark brown sugar** for the granulated sugar. Fold in 1½ cups shredded **carrots** (about 4 medium) and ½ cup **raisins** to the batter. Bake and cool as directed. Dust with **confectioners' sugar**.

**PER SERVING** 329 CAL, 15 G FAT (3 G SAT FAT), 45 MG CHOL, 185 MG SOD, 5 G PRO, 44 G CAR, 2 G FIBER

## ❹ *Almond-cranberry bread*

**ACTIVE** 15 MIN • **TOTAL** 1 HR 15 MIN PLUS COOLING • **SERVES** 10
**COST PER SERVING** 66¢

Prepare the basic quick bread with the following changes: Increase the **flour** to 2 cups and omit the cinnamon. Substitute 1 cup **sliced almonds** for the walnuts and ½ tsp **pure almond extract** for the vanilla extract. Fold in 1 cup **fresh** or **frozen cranberries** (chopped) to the batter. Transfer the batter to the baking pan and sprinkle the top with 2 Tbsp **sliced almonds**. Bake and cool as directed.

**PER SERVING** 365 CAL, 21 G FAT (4 G SAT FAT), 47 MG CHOL, 172 MG SOD, 6 G PRO, 38 G CAR, 2 G FIBER

# Sugar cookie switcheroo

Make four times the treats with a few simple tweaks to a sweet dough.

## BASIC SUGAR COOKIES

**ACTIVE** 25 MIN • **TOTAL** 40 MIN (PLUS CHILLING AND COOLING) • **MAKES** 50 • **COST PER COOKIE** 6¢

2¾    cups all-purpose flour

½    tsp baking powder

¼    tsp kosher salt

1    cup (2 sticks) unsalted butter, at room temperature

¾    cup granulated sugar

1    large egg

1½    tsp pure vanilla extract

**1** In a large bowl, whisk together the flour, baking powder and salt.

**2** Using an electric mixer, beat the butter and sugar until light and fluffy, about 3 minutes. Beat in the egg and then the vanilla.

**3** Reduce the mixer speed to low and gradually add the flour mixture, mixing just until incorporated. Shape the dough into 4 disks and roll each between 2 sheets of wax paper to ⅛-in. thick. Chill until firm, 30 minutes in the refrigerator or 15 minutes in the freezer.

**4** Heat oven to 350°F. Line baking sheets with parchment paper. Using floured cookie cutters, cut out cookies and place them on the prepared baking sheets. Reroll, chill and cut the scraps.

**5** Bake, rotating the positions of the pans halfway through, until the cookies are lightly golden brown around the edges, 10 to 12 minutes. Let cool on the sheets for 5 minutes before transferring to wire racks to cool completely.

**PER COOKIE** 72 CAL, 4 G FAT (2 G SAT FAT), 13 MG CHOL, 17 MG SOD, 1 G PRO, 8 G CAR, 0 G FIBER

### ① Brown sugar-ginger snowflakes

**ACTIVE** 45 MIN • **TOTAL** 55 MIN (PLUS CHILLING AND COOLING) • **MAKES** 36
**COST PER COOKIE** 10¢

When preparing the basic sugar cookies, reduce the **granulated sugar** to ¼ cup and add ½ cup firmly packed **dark brown sugar** and 2 tsp grated **fresh ginger** when beating the butter and sugar together. Roll, cut out with snowflake-shaped cutters, bake and let cool as directed. In a medium bowl, stir together 2 cups **confectioners' sugar** and 2 Tbsp **whole milk** until smooth. If desired, tint the icing blue. Transfer the icing to a piping bag fitted with a small round tip and pipe patterns on the cooled cookies. While the icing is wet, sprinkle with **sanding sugar**, if desired.

**PER COOKIE** 126 CAL, 5 G FAT (3 G SAT FAT), 19 MG CHOL, 25 MG SOD, 1 G PRO, 18 G CAR, 0 G FIBER

## ② *Jam sandwiches*

**ACTIVE** 35 MIN • **TOTAL** 50 MIN
(PLUS CHILLING AND COOLING)
**MAKES** 4 DOZEN • **COST PER COOKIE** 10¢

Prepare the basic sugar cookie dough and cut out using 2-in.-round fluted cutters. Using a smaller cutter, cut out the centers of half the cookies. Bake and cool as directed. Dust the cutout cookies with **confectioners' sugar**. Spread each of the whole cookies with 1½ tsp **apricot**, **orange** or **raspberry jam** and sandwich with the cutouts.

**PER COOKIE** 107 CAL, 4 G FAT (3 G SAT FAT), 15 MG CHOL, 23 MG SOD, 1 G PRO, 17 G CAR, 0 G FIBER

## ③ *Lime & coconut coins*

**ACTIVE** 35 MIN • **TOTAL** 50 MIN
(PLUS CHILLING AND COOLING)
**MAKES** 10 DOZEN • **COST PER COOKIE** 4¢

Prepare the basic sugar cookie dough and shape into 1½-in.-diameter logs. Wrap and freeze for 20 minutes. Slice into ⅛-in.-thick rounds and place on parchment-lined baking sheets. Bake and cool as directed. In a small bowl, whisk together 2 cups **confectioners' sugar**, ¼ cup **fresh lime juice** and 2 tsp grated **lime zest**. Spoon the glaze over each cookie, then sprinkle with toasted **shredded coconut** and let the cookies set.

**PER COOKIE** 36 CAL, 2 G FAT (1 G SAT FAT), 5 MG CHOL, 8 MG SOD, 0 G PRO, 5 G CAR, 0 G FIBER

## ④ *Minty chocolate-dipped candy canes*

**ACTIVE** 35 MIN • **TOTAL** 50 MIN
(PLUS CHILLING AND COOLING)
**MAKES** 5 DOZEN • **COST PER COOKIE** 8¢

Prepare the basic sugar cookie dough and cut out using candy cane–shape cutters. Bake and cool as directed. Melt 4 oz **semisweet** or **white chocolate** according to package directions, then stir in ¼ tsp **peppermint extract**. Dip half of each cookie in the chocolate, letting any excess drip off. Place on a cooling rack set over parchment paper and sprinkle with red and white **nonpareils** while wet.

**PER COOKIE** 70 CAL, 4 G FAT (2 G SAT FAT), 10 MG CHOL, 13 MG SOD, 1 G PRO, 8 G CAR, 0 G FIBER

# The big apple

No matter what your skill level, there's an apple pie here that you can master.

START HERE

## BASIC FLAKY PIE CRUST

**ACTIVE** 30 MIN • **TOTAL** 1 HR 30 MIN • **MAKES** 1 PIE CRUST

1¼ cups all-purpose flour

1 Tbsp granulated sugar

½ tsp kosher salt

½ cup (1 stick) cold unsalted butter, cut into small pieces

1 Tbsp white vinegar

1 to 2 Tbsp ice-cold water

**1** In a food processor, combine the flour, sugar and salt. Add the butter and pulse until the mixture resembles coarse crumbs.

**2** Add the vinegar and 1 Tbsp cold water, pulsing until the dough is crumbly but holds together when squeezed (if necessary, add the remaining water, 1 tsp at a time). Do not overmix.

**3** Transfer the dough to a piece of plastic wrap and shape into a 1-in.-thick disk. Wrap tightly and refrigerate until firm, at least 1 hour and up to 2 days.

**4** Roll and fill as directed.

# 1 Rustic apple pie

**ACTIVE** 45 MIN • **TOTAL** 1 HR 45 MIN PLUS COOLING • **SERVES** 8 • **COST PER SERVING** 70¢

- 1 Basic Flaky Pie crust
- 2 lb Jonagold, Idared or Golden Delicious apples (about 4 large), peeled and slice ½ in thick
- 1 lb Granny Smith apples (about 2 large), peeled and sliced ½ in. thick
- 1 Tbsp all-purpose flour
- 1 tsp orange zest
- ¼ tsp ground cinnamon
- ⅛ tsp freshly grated or ground nutmeg
- 3 Tbsp granulated sugar
- 1 large egg, slightly beaten

❶ Heat oven to 375°F. Working on a piece of parchment paper, roll the disk of dough into a 15-in. circle. Slide the paper (and crust) onto a baking sheet.

❷ In a large bowl, toss together the apples, flour, zest, cinnamon, nutmeg and 2 Tbsp sugar. Pile the apples on top of the crust, leaving a 3-in. border. Fold the border over the apples.

❸ Brush the crust with the egg. Sprinkle the entire pie with the remaining Tbsp sugar and bake until the crust is golden brown and the apples are tender, 55 to 65 minutes. Let stand for at least 30 minutes before serving. Serve warm or at room temperature.

**PER SERVING** 459 CAL, 24 G FAT (15 G SAT FAT), 84 MG CHOL, 254 MG SOD, 6 G PRO, 57 G CAR, 3 G FIBER

# ❷ *Apple & oatmeal-ginger crumb pie*

**ACTIVE** 50 MIN • **TOTAL** 2 HR 30 MIN PLUS COOLING • **SERVES** 8 • **COST PER SERVING** 84¢

1   Basic Flaky Pie crust

¼   cup firmly packed dark brown sugar

1   Tbsp freshly grated ginger or 1½ tsp ground ginger

½   tsp ground cinnamon

    Pinch kosher salt

1   cup all-purpose flour

½   cup (1 stick) cold unsalted butter, cut into small pieces

1   cup old-fashioned rolled oats

2   lb Jonagold, Idared or Golden Delicious apples (about 4 large), peeled and sliced ½ in. thick

1   lb Granny Smith apples (about 2 large), peeled and sliced ½ in. thick

2   Tbsp fresh lemon juice

½   cup granulated sugar

1   Tbsp cornstarch

❶ Heat oven to 375°F. On a lightly floured surface, roll the disk of dough into a 12-in. circle. Fit it into the bottom and up the sides of a 9-in. pie plate. If necessary, trim the dough so the overhang is even all the way around (about ½ in. from the edge of the pie plate). Fold the overhang under itself to create a thicker rim of dough and crimp as desired. Refrigerate until ready to fill.

❷ In a food processor, pulse the brown sugar, ginger, cinnamon and salt to combine. Add the flour and pulse to incorporate. Add the butter and pulse just until the mixture forms large clumps. Transfer to a bowl and gently toss with the oats; refrigerate until ready to use.

❸ In a large bowl, toss the apples with the lemon juice. Add the granulated sugar and cornstarch and toss to coat. Transfer the apples to the pie crust. Top with the crumb mixture and bake for 1 hour. Cover with foil and bake until the apples are tender (use a wooden pick to check doneness) and the topping is golden brown, 18 to 22 minutes more. Let stand for at least 1 hour before serving. Serve warm or at room temperature.

**PER SERVING** 526 CAL, 24 G FAT (15 G SAT FAT), 61 MG CHOL, 141 MG SOD, 6 G PRO, 74 G CAR, 4 G FIBER

# ③ *Brown sugar-pecan apple pie*

**ACTIVE** 1 HR 15 MIN • **TOTAL** 2 HR 45 MIN PLUS COOLING • **SERVES** 8 • **COST PER SERVING** $1.38

- 2   Tbsp unsalted butter
- 2   lb Jonagold, Idared or Golden Delicious apples (about 4 large), peeled and sliced ½ in thick
- 2   lb Granny Smith apples (about 4 large), peeled and sliced ½ in. thick
- ¾   cup plus 1 Tbsp firmly packed dark brown sugar
- 1   Tbsp cornstarch
- 1   cup pecans, broken into pieces
- 1   tsp pure vanilla extract
- 2   Basic Flaky Pie crusts
- 2   large eggs, beaten
- 1   Tbsp raw sugar
- ¼   tsp kosher salt
- 1   2-in. leaf cookie cutter

❶ Melt the butter in a large, straight-sided skillet over medium-high heat. Add the apples and ¾ cup brown sugar and cook, tossing occasionally, until just tender, 8 to 10 minutes.

❷ In a small bowl, combine the cornstarch and the remaining Tbsp brown sugar. Sprinkle over the apples and cook until thickened, about 1 minute. Remove from heat, add the pecans and vanilla and toss to combine. Let cool, tossing occasionally, to room temperature, about 40 minutes.

❸ Heat oven to 375°F. On a lightly floured surface, roll one disk of dough into a 12-in. circle. Fit it into the bottom and up the sides of a 9-in. pie plate. Trim the overhang to ½ in. all the way around. Refrigerate until ready to use.

❹ Working on a floured piece of parchment paper, roll the remaining disk of dough into a 12-in. circle. Using a 2-in. leaf cookie cutter and starting 1½ in. from the edge, cut out 1 row of 4 leaves directly in the center of the crust, spacing them ½ in. apart. Cut out additional leaves around the first row, spacing them ½ in. apart and leaving a 1½-in. border along the edge (figure on about 22 leaves total). Refrigerate the cut out dough. Using a wooden pick or knife, score lines into the leaves.

❺ Spoon the cooled filling into the crust in the pie plate and carefully place or slide the chilled cutout crust on top, being careful not to stretch the dough. Trim the top crust to ¾ in. from the edge of the pie plate. Fold the top crust under the bottom crust to create a thicker crust to seal; crimp as desired.

❻ Brush the entire pie with some of the egg and sprinkle with the raw sugar and salt. Brush the undersides of the leaf cutouts with some of the egg and place them around the edge of the pie, gently pressing to help them adhere. Brush the tops of the leaves with the remaining egg and bake until the crust is golden brown, 50 to 55 minutes. Let cool to room temperature before serving.

**PER SERVING** 667 CAL, 36 G FAT (18 G SAT FAT), 92 MG CHOL, 321 MG SOD, 7 G PRO, 84 G CAR, 5 G FIBER

## MEASUREMENT CONVERSION CHART

| | | | |
|---|---|---|---|
| pinch/dash | ¹⁄₁₆ teaspoon | | |
| 1 teaspoon | | | |
| ½ Tablespoon | 1½ teaspoons | ¼ fl oz | 7.5 ml |
| 1 Tablespoon | 3 teaspoons | ½ fl oz | 15 ml |
| ¼ cup | 4 Tablespoons | 2 fl oz | 60 ml |
| ⅓ cup | 5 Tablespoons + 1 teaspoon | 2½ fl oz | 75 ml |
| ½ cup | 8 Tablespoons | 4 fl oz | 120 ml |
| ⅔ cup | 10 Tablespoons + 2 teaspoons | 5 fl oz | 150 ml |
| ¾ cup | 12 Tablespoons | 6 fl oz | 180 ml |
| 1 cup | 16 Tablespoons or ½ pint | 8 fl oz | 240 ml |
| 1 pint | 2 cups | 16 fl oz | 475 ml |
| 1 quart | 2 pints or 4 cups | 32 fl oz | 945 ml |
| 1 gallon | 4 quarts or 16 cups | 128 fl oz | 3.8 liters |
| 1 pound | 16 ounces | | |

## WHEN IS IT DONE?

The most accurate way to tell when meat and poultry are done is to use an instant-read thermometer. To the right lists the *Woman's Day* test kitchen's preference (and considered safe by many food experts and chefs) for tender and juicy results.

\* The U.S. Department of Agriculture recommends cooking beef, pork and lamb to a minimum internal temperature of 145°F and poultry to 165°F for maximum food safety.

| BEEF | WD TEST KITCHEN |
|---|---|
| Rare | 118°F* |
| Medium-rare | 125°F–130°F* |
| Medium | 135°F–140°F* |
| Medium-well | 150°F |
| Well-done | 155°F |

| LAMB | |
|---|---|
| Medium-rare | 125°F–130°F* |
| Medium | 140°F* |
| Medium-well | 150°F |
| Well-done | 155°F |

| PORK | |
|---|---|
| | 145°F |

| POULTRY | |
|---|---|
| White Meat | 160°F* |
| Dark Meat | 165°F |

## TEMPERATURE CONVERSION CHART

| °F | °C |
|---|---|
| 225°F | 110°C |
| 250°F | 125°C |
| 275°F | 135°C |
| 300°F | 150°C |
| 325°F | 160°C |
| 350°F | 175°C |
| 375°F | 190°C |
| 400°F | 200°C |
| 425°F | 220°C |
| 450°F | 230°C |

♥ For the nutritional criteria that make our recipes heart-healthy go to *womansday.com/hhcriteria*.

# GENERAL INDEX

## INDEX BY CATEGORY

## ACKNOWLEDGEMENTS

There are so many steps that go into producing the recipes you see in these pages and so many people who are integral to their success.

Special thanks to the those who worked together to come up with ideas and develop recipes. And to those who joined us in the test kitchen tweaking and adjusting to ensure each recipe's ease and deliciousness: Anna Helm Baxter, Janine Desiderio, Jo Keohane, Sue Li, Donna Meadow, Brett Regot, Yasmin Sabir, Hadas Smirnoff, Chelsea Zimmer

Thank you to the teams that came together for photo shoots. Along with photographers, these food stylists, prop stylists and art directors help make our food look as good as it tastes: Isabel Abdai, Simon Andrews, Anna Helm Baxter, Philippa Brathwaite, Cindy Diprima, Anne Disrude, Molly Fitzsimons, Matthew Gleason, Megan Hedgpeth, Paige Hicks, Vivian Liu, Marina Malchin, Cyd McDowell, Donna Meadow, Frank Mentesana, Pam Morris, Carrie Purcell, Maggie Ruggiero, Sara Quesenberry, Hadas Smirnoff, Erin Swift, Victor Thompson, Alistair Turnbull, Gerri Williams, Michelle Wong.

## PHOTO CREDITS

**Lucas Allen** 8
**Antonis Achilleos** 32, 47, 48, 49, 114, 117, 118, 119
**Iain Bagwell** 10, 32, 81, 82, 83, 88, 92, 114, 125, 126, 127, 133, 134, 137
**Levi Brown** 32, 39, 40
**Steve Giralt** 10, 25, 26, 27
**John Kernick** 32, 73, 74
**Maura McEvoy** 77, 78, 79
**Johnny Miller** 88, 99, 100, 107, 108, 109, 110, 111, 112
**Kana Okada** 10, 21, 22, 23, 29, 30, 43, 44, 45, 52, 54, 55, 61, 62, 63, 64
**Con Poulos** 32, 57, 58, 85, 86, 87, 95, 96
**Alexandra Rowley** 32, 65, 66
**Kate Sears** 114, 129, 130,
**Kat Teutsch** 32, 69, 70, 71, 114, 121, 122,
**Mark Thomas** 10, 17, 17
**Jonny Valiant**
**Sarah Anne Ward** 88, 103, 104, 105
**Michael Waring** 7
**Romulo Yanes** 32, 35, 36, 37, 50, 51

FRONT COVER
**Ian Bagwell**

BACK COVER
**Mark Thomas, Ian Bagwell, Ian Bagwell**

FLAP
**Kat Teutsch, Kat Teutsch, Con Poulos, Con Poulos**

HEARST BOOKS
New York

An Imprint of Sterling Publishing
387 Park Avenue South
New York, NY 10016

Every effort has been made to ensure that all the information in this book is accurate. However, due
to differing conditions, tools, and individual skills, the publisher cannot be responsible for any injuries,
losses, and/or other damages that may result from the use of the information in this book.

..............................

Editor-in-Chief Susan Spencer
Creative Director Sara Williams
Art Director Isabel Abdai
Executive Editor Annemarie Conte
Food & Nutrition Director Kate Merker
Senior Associate Food Editor Yasmin Sabir
Associate Food Editor Anna Helm Baxter
Copy Editor Lauren Spencer

..............................

ISBN 978-1-61837-142-3

Distributed in Canada by Sterling Publishing
C/o Canadian Manda Group, 165 Dufferin Street
Toronto, Ontario, Canada M6K 3H6
Distributed in the United Kingdom by GMC Distribution Services
Castle Place, 166 High Street, Lewes, East Sussex, England BN7 1XU
Distributed in Australia by Capricorn Link (Australia) Pty. Ltd.
P.O. Box 704, Windsor, NSW 2756, Australia

For information about custom editions, special sales, and premium and corporate purchases,
please contact Sterling Special Sales at 800-805-5489 or specialsales@sterlingpublishing.com.

Manufactured in China

2  4  6  8  10  9  7  5  3  1

www.sterlingpublishing.com